TAXES 101

FROM **UNDERSTANDING FORMS** AND **FILING** TO **USING TAX LAWS** AND **POLICIES** TO **MINIMIZE COSTS** AND **MAXIMIZE WEALTH**, AN **ESSENTIAL PRIMER ON THE US TAX SYSTEM**

MICHELE CAGAN, CPA

ADAMS MEDIA

NEW YORK   LONDON   TORONTO   SYDNEY   NEW DELHI

To Shine, who learned more about taxes
than they ever wanted to know.

Adams Media
An Imprint of Simon & Schuster, LLC
100 Technology Center Drive
Stoughton, Massachusetts 02072

First Adams Media hardcover edition
November 2024

ADAMS MEDIA and colophon are registered
trademarks of Simon & Schuster, LLC.

Simon & Schuster: Celebrating
100 Years of Publishing in 2024

For information about special discounts
for bulk purchases, please contact Simon &
Schuster Special Sales at 1-866-506-1949 or
business@simonandschuster.com.

The Simon & Schuster Speakers Bureau can
bring authors to your live event. For more
information or to book an event, contact the
Simon & Schuster Speakers Bureau at 1-866-
248-3049 or visit our website at
www.simonspeakers.com.

Manufactured in the United States of America

1 2024

Library of Congress Cataloging-in-
Publication Data
Names: Cagan, Michele, author.
Title: Taxes 101 / Michele Cagan, CPA.
Other titles: Taxes one hundred and one
Description: First Adams Media hardcover
edition. | Stoughton, Massachusetts: Adams
Media, 2024. | Series: Adams 101 series |
Includes index.
Identifiers: LCCN 2024024490 | ISBN
9781507222652 (hc) | ISBN 9781507222669
(ebook)
Subjects: LCSH: Taxation--United States.
Classification: LCC HJ2362 .C34 2024 |
DDC 343.7304--dc23/eng/20240614
LC record available at https://lccn.loc
.gov/2024024490

ISBN 978-1-5072-2265-2
ISBN 978-1-5072-2266-9 (ebook)

CONTENTS

INTRODUCTION

You may not realize it, but taxes are probably one of your largest expenses. Between income taxes, sales taxes, property taxes, and others, this cost eats somewhere between 30% and 50% of the average American's income. That said, you're probably not even aware how much of your total paycheck goes toward these different taxes.

Unfortunately, paying taxes is a way of life, but in *Taxes 101* you'll learn that the amount of money you pay doesn't have to be unsettling. In fact, there are a lot of things you can do to manage and minimize your tax burden. That doesn't just apply to income taxes—you can use certain strategies to reduce virtually every kind of tax you have to pay. Throughout this book, you'll learn helpful information like:

- What common forms you'll need to fill out during tax season
- How taxes evolved into their current form
- How the US tax code works and what influences it
- What the different types of personal taxes are
- How to estimate your taxes
- What steps to take to handle issues with the Internal Revenue Service (IRS)
- And more!

Each section throughout this book will bring you closer to understanding how taxes work. Plus, you'll get current, real-world examples to illustrate the harder-to-grasp economic examples. For example, you'll learn how our latest presidents tackled changes in tax law, how to deal with a potential case of identity theft (which is becoming more and more common), and the taxes associated with starting a new business. With each real-world example, you'll be able to apply what you've learned throughout these pages to your economic life—and you'll watch your wallet grow as you do!

No matter your financial standing, *Taxes 101* will help you understand the laws, theories, and history of taxes, while you reap the financial benefits. Let's begin!

Chapter 1

History of Taxation

Taxes came about when rulers, local and national, needed more than they could produce or earn themselves. Anywhere a ruler or ruling party emerged, taxes soon followed. Rather than waiting to be paid, they took taxes from their subjects, collecting the best of the harvest or the finest oxen. In the earliest days, many taxes were paid with personal labor or military service. Anything the ruler needed could be turned into a tax—not just currency.

Those first taxes were based on property rather than income but soon evolved to include the first sales, income, trade, and inheritance taxes. Rulers created taxes on merchants and nomads crossing their lands or waterways. Merchants were taxed on the goods they sold, and the purchasers later taxed on the goods they had bought. Many times, the people were left nearly impoverished as the ruling classes took whatever share they wanted. In other cases, leaders imposed taxes more fairly, never leaving their people in want, and providing services in return, rather than only armed protection against invaders. Though taxes emerged all around the world, they took different shapes in different areas.

ANCIENT TAXES

Donkeys, Soap, and Cucumbers

Taxes from ancient times varied as much as the different civilizations imposing them. The tax laws from each of these places drew from the laws that had been established before them, and many of the principles have lasted into modern-day use. In many cases, tax collections involved both goods and services. Goods included everything from oxen to olive oil to the currency of the time. Levied services often included military responsibilities, but also service to the community at large.

GREECE: BRAGGING ABOUT TAXES

Only the wealthiest citizens of ancient Athens paid voluntary taxes, considering the payment to be a sign of social status that came with bragging rights. Wealthy individuals actually competed to pay more than their peers. Those taxes funded the city-state's essential expenses, primarily its navy and tributes to the gods. The Athenian navy was extensive and expensive, requiring triremes (huge wooden warships) to be built and manned. The wealthiest citizens volunteered to sponsor those ships and their crews, often commanding the ships themselves, in exchange for recognition of their fortunes and good works.

Another part of the system was called liturgies, which funded public works projects including support for the arts and construction of gymnasiums. The wealthy believed that paying liturgies was well worth the social capital reward. Depending on the needs of the Athenian government, there were anywhere between a few hundred and more than a thousand liturgists in the city-state. A main benefit of this system involved more than taxes paid; liturgists generally managed the projects they funded, lending their expertise to the community and taking personal responsibility for doing the job well.

ROME: WIDESPREAD TAXATION

Ancient Rome was all about expansion, which required many troops and weapons for war, and therefore significant funds. Every newly conquered land was added to the kingdom and taxed accordingly.

One of its first levies was a harvest tax in exchange for "renting" public land. That was soon followed with a tax on merchants entering the land, requiring them to pay up to 5% of the value of the goods they brought in as a customs duty of sorts.

But the most widespread tax was based on social structure and territory. The sixth king of ancient Rome, Servius Tullius, divided the state into four urban and seventeen rural tribes (districts), the number of which increased with each conquest pursued. Tullius then introduced a property census and an estimation of population size. This census led to Roman society (adult men who owned property) being divided into five classes according to their status, wealth, and age; these classes were further divided into smaller groups that each consisted of one hundred men. The military duties that Roman men had to carry out varied based on this class division, but each class was required to contribute a specific number of soldiers and a *tributum*, a tax levied to help fund the ongoing wars.

As the kingdom transformed into the Roman Republic, its tax system transformed as well. Rome was the center of its own universe surrounded by vast conquered territories, and managing all of that required significant funding. The tributum system still taxed all real property, like land and buildings. Citizens continued to perform public duties, primarily military service, but these were levied on groups of people rather than individuals. The biggest change was the introduction of provinces, conquered lands whose people were not considered Roman citizens. Tax responsibilities and rates differed by province, and some were even completely exempted from taxation. The most privileged province was Sicily, as Sicilian bread was essential for the citizens and the army.

Provincial taxes included road tolls, fees for donkey tags, inheritance taxes, a tax on cucumbers, fees for the erection of statues, fees for the maintenance of famous guests, and soap taxes.

As Rome had a larger population and thus a large military to support, tax collections continually increased, as did the number of different taxes.

The Weirdest Tax: *Vectigal Urinae*

In the Roman Empire, urine was a prized commodity used for producing chemicals like ammonia. Because of its value, people collected and sold urine reclaimed from public toilets. So, Emperor Nero introduced a urine tax, the *vectigal urinae*, to cash in on this lucrative trade.

CHINA:
THE BEGINNING OF TAX BRACKETS

Recent archaeological discoveries let to a surprising tax find: Ancient inked bamboo slips indicate that the earliest Chinese taxes used a bracket system, where people with less paid less tax. Tax levies changed annually due to various factors like weather and crop yields and even exempting farmers whose land didn't produce that year. The goal of this system was to preserve fairness and to avoid undue burdens on people who didn't have the means to pay.

INDIA: FOCUSED ON FAIRNESS

Ancient India hosted a diverse population and the tax system was especially varied. Its tax system is codified in the *Arthashastra*, a Sanskrit treatise on governing strategies with heavy emphasis on financial and tax matters. Most taxes were based on the production yields from agriculture, metal mining, and forestry. A salt tax was one of the largest revenue sources, with the tax collected where the salt was mined. There were also land and water taxes, tolls, and a variety of duties associated with local businesses. Taxes could be paid with gold coins, grains, raw materials, cattle, or personal service.

India also relied heavily on trade with China and other countries in the immediate area. They imposed a special levy called *vartanam* on goods imported into India, as well as a *dvarodaya* tax on the import businesses themselves.

While it seems like everyone and everything were taxed, the guiding principle in this system was fairness. The kingdom did collect taxes from every possible source, but it made sure that the citizens did not feel overburdened by taxes. The relationship was a fair trade: The kingdom provided support and protection, while the subjects provided tax revenues. If the subjects felt they were not being served, they could refuse to pay or demand refunds of their taxes. The overarching goal was a prosperous, safe society where everyone paid a fair share.

MESOAMERICA:
CHARGING CHOCOLATE

As far back as 1750 B.C.E. in Mesoamerica (modern-day Mexico and Central America), cacao beans were used as currency in place of coins. The ancient Aztecs and Mayans placed a high value on chocolate, so much so that it was a primary means of paying taxes. Hundreds of works of art depict cacao being used to pay tributes and taxes.

The Aztecs had a unique tax system for the time, particularly at the city-state level. Their culture focused more on the routine collection of taxes rather than tributes, which were more haphazard and required some form of recognition in return for payment. Government officials and nobles did not have to pay any taxes, but common citizens paid tax in the form of labor and goods, including cacao beans.

In Mayan society, nobles and priests administered the city-states, collecting taxes and labor for local projects, including temple construction. Conquered states were also taxed to provide the Aztecs with precious metals, incense, paper, and chocolate. Additionally, in Mayan culture, pottery and canvases picture commodities like cacao beans, maize, and tobacco being delivered to leaders as payment for taxes and tributes. The Mayan kings considered dried cacao beans as currency, and they collected much more than the palace could consume, using the surplus for trade and troops.

TAXES TAKE HOLD IN EUROPE

You're Not Suggesting We Should Tax...Everything?

As civilizations progressed, tax systems evolved along with them. Plus, as nation-states solidified, particularly during the thirteenth century, taxation grew with the culture.

Increasing international trade brought more opportunities to tax. Wars demanded bigger national treasuries, leading to higher taxes on the people. During the Middle Ages and Renaissance, Europe was defined by military skirmishes, invasions, expanding empires, and religion. Clashes between church and state often involved some form of taxation (though it was not always called that).

At first, most tax systems were based on land and trade and were modeled from days when the Romans ruled, but as kingdoms needed more funding, they began turning to other sources for revenue. From Viking raids to the Hundred Years' War to the Crusades, major cultural movements dictated new tax policies across Europe.

VIKINGS AND THE DANEGELD

From the ninth through eleventh centuries, the Vikings traveled from Scandinavia into Europe primarily by sea. These well-known pirates, conquerors, and colonizers seized control of many territories and raided others. The seafaring Vikings inspired fear throughout Europe, as well as inspiring and demanding new taxes.

To protect the British Isles from constant attacks, King Ethelred II paid the Viking raiders thousands of pounds of silver along with regular tribute. That tribute, called Danegeld, became one of the first direct taxes levied in Europe. Each taxpayer in the land faced a Danegeld based on their income and property. Essentially, this tax was paid in exchange for protection against further Viking raids. The King would collect the tax and hand it over to the raiders to protect his land and people. One innovation of the time was the Domesday book, details from a national land survey conducted in 1085 that covered most of Great Britain, giving the kingdom information about landowners' properties and income. The Danegeld lasted for more than one hundred years and led to more than one hundred tons of silver being added to the Scandinavian coffers.

Lady Godiva and the Naked Ride

When the people of Coventry became impoverished due to crippling taxes, Lady Godiva persistently begged her husband, Leofric (Earl of Mercia), to lower the taxes and give them some relief. Leofric told his wife that he would lower taxes when she rode through town naked at midday. According to legend, she took that naked ride on horseback in protest and, honoring his word, the earl reduced taxes on the people of Coventry.

THE CRUSADES

The Crusades were a series of military expeditions during the Middle Ages initiated by the Church and undertaken by European Christians. For around two hundred years, Western European life was fixated on the Crusades as the Church tried to take over the Holy Land and stop the spread of Islam. The ultimately unsuccessful campaigns militarized Western Europe and the Church. The costs were enormous, requiring a steady inflow of taxes, setting the stage for more formal taxation in many European countries.

Venice supplied ships to the crusaders in exchange for payment and tax-free trading. When the kings of England and France ran short on funds, the Venetians had the crusaders attack their biggest rivals in trade around the Mediterranean (mainly parts of the Byzantine Empire). Venice gained territory along with half of the raids' loot.

The most famous such tax was known as the Saladin Tithe. Introduced by King Henry II, this tax for the English and Welsh was a straight 10% levy on all personal income and movable property, and it was used to fund the Church and the Crusades. The tithe was named for the famous Muslim hero and leader, Salah al-Din Yusuf ibn Ayyub (called Saladin by the English), who fought the crusaders in the Middle East. Later on, this tax practice was also adopted by King Philip II of France. Knights and clerics were generally exempted from paying this tax as a benefit of their status.

THE HUNDRED YEARS' WAR

Toward the end of the Middle Ages, war broke out between England and France. Despite the name, the Hundred Years' War was really a series of conflicts from 1337 to 1453 triggered by disputes about territory and the succession line to the French throne. It started when England's King Edward III invaded Flanders, claiming his right to the crown of France. The war drained both countries' treasuries, leading to increased taxation in England and France.

The on-and-off war caused widespread ruin. Farms were destroyed, tradesmen lost their livelihoods, and many lost their lives. This reduced the tax base, leading to further increased taxes and additional duties on English and French citizens. For a time, the English occupied northern France, imposing high taxes on the conquered. They captured France's King John II and demanded an exorbitant ransom of three million gold coins (called *ècus d'or*). To raise the ransom, the French imposed heavy tax burdens as well, leading to peasant uprisings.

THE SPANISH ALCABALA

One of the most hated early European taxes was the Spanish alcabala, a heavy sales tax imposed on the people of Spain and all of its territories. It was first introduced in 1342 with rates ranging from 1% to at least 10% depending on the product and its final destination in the production and sales chain, the end user. Plus, it covered a wide variety of common products like fish, bread, wine, oil, and clothing.

This taxation system led to a lot of workarounds, as people tried avoiding or minimizing the tax by sending goods to a low-tax locale and then using them somewhere else. Ultimately, the Spanish crown contracted with local tax farmers to handle collections and had trouble enforcing compliance. This trouble with enforcement combined with ongoing unsuccessful military initiatives led to economic decline.

FLORENCE'S ADVANCED FINANCES

Between its formation as the ancient Roman military colony Florentia and becoming the birthplace of the Renaissance, Florence transformed into an important financial center of medieval Europe.

Florence was a major trade destination that combined commerce and culture and thrived as an economic hub. The city's prosperity grew, leading to shifts in the means and methods of taxation.

Wealth shifted from being land-based toward more liquid capital, and taxes followed suit. Indirect excise taxes called gabelles were levied, and by the mid-1400s they were responsible for filling more than 75% of the public treasury, while land tax revenues declined. As Florence got drawn into wars, it turned to borrowing funds from citizens rather than raising taxes, often forcing the loans through the *Monte Comune* (a division that managed public debt).

To track its finances, the Florentine government created advanced organizational systems for record-keeping. They developed bookkeeping practices and the *Catasto,* a detailed system for land and property registration. The information in the *Catasto* helped the rulers levy a tax (originally 1%, but it varied over the years) on citizens' wealth.

BRITISH EMPIRE AND AMERICAN REVOLUTION

The Taxes-Tea Commotion

The 1700s marked an era of both economic and geographic expansion for Great Britain, giving birth to the British Empire. During this time, the Industrial Revolution was underway, leading to significant changes in the way important commodities were produced. With their unmatched naval fleet projecting power and merchant fleet dominating trade, the British Empire became one of history's mightiest empires.

At its most powerful, the British Empire controlled nearly 25% of the world's land and people. It spanned from North America to Asia to Australia to Africa. Safeguarding its vast territories, protectorates, and colonies was an enormous—and expensive—undertaking. So, the British Parliament began taxing everything and everyone.

THE BRITISH TAX EVERYTHING

In the mid- to late-1700s, the British government had to pay the lavish costs associated with expanding an empire and fighting wars (like the Napoleonic Wars with France). Enter Prime Minister William Pitt, who introduced tax after tax on the British people. Some of these taxes were very short-lived due to protests and workarounds, while others stuck around. Here are just a few of the taxes introduced during that time:

- **The Duties on Clocks and Watches Act** charged an annual tax on basic watches, gold watches, and clocks. To avoid the tax, people simply got rid of or hid their timepieces. They turned to local taverns to find out what time it was, and the tavern owners happily displayed huge decorative clocks to attract more patrons. The clock and watch industry suffered, people lost jobs, and the easy workarounds led to very little tax being collected. This tax was repealed only nine months after it was instituted.
- **The Hat Tax** was the British government's solution for a simple way to raise revenues. The theory was that wealthy men would own many expensive hats, and therefore pay more taxes than poor men, who could afford only one or two. Hat sellers were forced to pay for licenses, and all men's hats were required to have revenue stamps on their linings. Both milliners and their customers faced heavy fines if they did not pay the hat tax. Plus, those forging hat tax revenue stamps faced the threat of the death penalty.

Not wanting to leave a single tax unturned, Pitt's government-imposed taxes on virtually everything, including gold and silver plates, hair powder, wallpaper, perfume, brick, gloves, windows, beer, and soap. But even still, the government wasn't raising enough revenues to maintain the British Empire. So, they shifted their taxation focus to the colonies.

THE CROWN TAXES THE COLONISTS

To stake their claim on the New World, and then run it the way they saw fit, the British sent a large army to North America. It cost England huge sums of money to govern the American colonies, so they taxed the colonists heavily to pay for the cost. The British consistently imposed a variety of new taxes during the mid-1700s including:

- **The Sugar Act** was designed to make it harder for the colonists to engage in trade with any country other than England. It took effect in September 1764 and imposed high duties on foreign refined sugar and other foreign imports like wine and coffee. The Sugar Act had an enormous impact on colonists in New England, where creating rum from sugar was a key industry.
- **The Currency Act** was passed by the British Parliament in 1764, and it prohibited colonial governments from printing and issuing paper money. This Act was passed to support British merchants who felt being paid in colonial currency shortchanged them. This new law was not strictly about taxes, but it made it even harder for the colonists to pay their taxes to the crown.
- **The Stamp Act**, officially called "An Act for Granting and Applying Certain Stamp Duties," was passed in March 1765 and taxed all documents circulating in the colonies, including newspapers. It imposed a penny tax on every sheet of paper the colonists used.
- **The Quartering Act** of 1765 technically didn't impose a new monetary tax on the colonists. Instead, it required them to pay for food and lodging for British soldiers. It also gave royal governors the authority to dictate where British soldiers would be quartered, removing that power from colonial legislatures.

The Parliament passed and enacted the Townshend Acts, which triggered additional taxes on items like glass, paper, and tea. As a result, the colonists resisted those new taxes in ways the British government had not anticipated.

THE AMERICAN COLONISTS RESPOND ANGRILY

After years of struggling under the heavy taxation demanded by England, the colonists began to resist and rebel. The passing of the Tea Act in 1773 was one of the final straws that eventually led to revolution. The Tea Act effectively edged colonial tea sellers out of the trade in favor of the British East India Company, making the early Americans furious.

In protest, a group of colonists dumped 342 chests of tea belonging to the East India Company into Boston Harbor. They would no longer stand for taxation without representation. Parliament imposed the Coercive Acts of 1774 (called the Intolerable Acts in the colonies), which were composed of four punitive measures in retaliation. England effectively closed down the harbor until the tea was paid for, replaced the elective government with appointees, increased the power of the military governor, and forced quartering for the royal military.

These demonstrations of power were supposed to get the colonists to fall back in line. But they backfired, instead uniting the colonists against the crown. And the seeds of the American Revolution were firmly planted.

Star Wars: A Tale about Taxes

A long time ago in a galaxy far, far away… Taxation of trade routes led to revolution. The Galactic Senate imposed these taxes over the objections of the Trade Federation. That led to the complete blockade of Naboo, which would only be lifted if the taxes were repealed.

THE US STARTS IMPOSING TAXES

We'll Take Your Money Now

Though the Revolutionary War was spurred from discontentment with taxes, it was actually about representation. Without financial and other support from England, the leaders of the American colonies knew that they would need to increase their own taxes. When the United States first came together and created the Constitution, one of the first orders of business was giving Congress the power to impose taxes on the people.

They started with tariffs, moved to excise taxes, tried (and eventually failed) to impose land and property taxes, and eventually initiated income taxes. Throughout the years, taxes have changed dramatically, both in amount and scope.

TARIFFS AND EXCISE TAXES

Until the Constitution was ratified, the federal government didn't have the power to raise any revenues on its own. After it was in place, federal funds were raised mainly through tariffs and excise taxes, typically administered and remitted by the states.

The new nation desperately needed funds since it had heavily borrowed to finance the Revolutionary War and also needed to finance the everyday expenses of running the country. In 1789, Congress passed three bills to address their lopsided budget:

- The Tariff Act imposed duties on goods imported into the United States.

- The Duties on Tonnage statute imposed duties on vessels based on their capacity.
- Regulation of the Duties on Tonnage and on Merchandise established the United States Custom Service, and a way to collect those duties.

These were soon followed by the first excise taxes. The first was an excise tax on whiskey, implemented by Treasury Secretary Alexander Hamilton in 1791. This tax faced a lot of opposition, leading to the Whiskey Rebellion. President Washington sent in nearly 13,000 troops and squashed the rebellion, establishing the authority to impose such taxes. After that, the federal government added additional excise taxes on tobacco, sugar, gunpowder, and (yes) tea.

More tariffs and taxes were introduced over the next decades, some with the primary goal of raising revenues and others with different aims, such as protecting US merchants from foreign competition. For example, the Dallas Tariff (also called the Tariff of 1816) levied a 25% tax on cotton and wool products imported into the country. It served the double job of fattening the federal budget and benefiting local producers and merchants.

Tariffs versus Excise Taxes

Tariffs and excise taxes are both imposed on goods, but in different ways. Tariffs, also called duties, are levied on imported items. Excise taxes are levied on the manufacture and distribution of certain goods, typically those considered non-essential.

INCOME TAXES FUND
THE CIVIL WAR

The Civil War set the stage for seismic changes in America, including the first federal income tax. To fund the Union army, the country borrowed heavily, sold public lands, and doubled down on collecting existing taxes. When that wasn't enough, the House Ways and Means Committee wrote a bill to initiate an income tax on both citizens and corporations. Though this initial bill wouldn't go into effect despite quick passage, it paved the way for a follow-up bill that was signed into law in 1862.

The first official federal income tax imposed a 3% income tax on earnings between $600 and $10,000 and a 5% tax on higher earnings. When that proved to fall short for the war-funding needs, the House Ways and Means Committee amended the law in 1864 to increase the tax rate and add another layer: 5% on incomes between $600 and $5,000, 7.5% on incomes between $5,000 and $10,000, and 10% on all higher earnings.

Within just ten years, the income tax law was repealed by Congress. Later attempts to restore federal income tax collection were declared unconstitutional and struck down by the Supreme Court in 1895 (even though the Court had upheld the tax during the war). Their reasoning: The Constitution stated that any direct tax had to be proportionally divided among the states based on population. Until, that is, the Sixteenth Amendment to the Constitution came to be.

THE SIXTEENTH AMENDMENT

The Sixteenth Amendment to the Constitution was passed on July 2, 1909, and ratified on February 3, 1913. It gave Congress the authority to impose federal income taxes, which would eventually become the primary source of revenue for the federal government. The Amendment states, "The Congress shall have power to lay and collect taxes on incomes, from whatever source derived, without apportionment among the several States, and without regard to any census or enumeration."

Once this amendment was adopted, revenue collection in the United States underwent a major change. Corporate income taxes were levied almost immediately after the passage, though they were repealed just a few years later. Individual income taxes were implemented to help fund World War I efforts in 1913. All taxpayers paid the same progressive rates (ranging from 1% to 7%) on their income; there weren't yet any filing statuses, like single or married. With a slate of generous deductions and exemptions, only about 1% of the population paid any income taxes then, mostly at the lowest possible rate of 1%.

INCOME TAXES THROUGH THE YEARS

Tax rates and tax rules changed dramatically over time. The Revenue Act of 1942 introduced deductions for medical and investment expenses, and The Current Tax Payment Act (1943) introduced withholding taxes. Plus, The Individual Income Tax Act (1944) introduced the standard deduction, and The Revenue Act of 1948 introduced the married filing jointly tax status.

In addition to rule changes, tax rates and tax brackets have varied widely. The highest tax rate ever was 94% in 1944, for example. And while there were only two tax brackets in 1913, there were twelve in 1976 (it has since decreased to seven, as of 2024).

CONGRESS CREATES NEW TAXES

Always looking for ways to increase revenues, Congress has created other types of taxes since they were first empowered to do so. Two of the most important include estate taxes and FICA taxes.

The Stamp Act of 1797 launched the first estate-based taxes attaching duties to transfers of wealth. That version was repealed in 1802, but estate taxes cropped up again. The version in place today began in 1916. That law was reshaped a few times between 1976 and 1986 and was eventually phased out by 2010, only to reappear in full force in 2011.

Social Security and Medicare taxes entered the scene at different times but eventually came together under the Federal Insurance Contributions Act (FICA). The Social Security Act of 1935 introduced the concept, and the first Social Security taxes were collected from workers in 1937. The Medicare and Medicaid Act was signed into law in 1965, and Medicare taxes were first withheld in 1966. Both fall under FICA.

WHERE YOUR TAX DOLLARS GO

I'm Paying for What?!

Have you ever wondered what exactly the government is doing with the taxes you pay? Millions of Americans wonder that every year, and the answers are easier to find than you might think. The Internal Revenue Service (IRS) collects your money, but they're not the ones that disburse it. That's decided by Congress, often with guidance from the president. And while many federal government expenses won't surprise you, others will have you shaking your head in disbelief.

THE CONGRESSIONAL BUDGET ACT

The Congressional Budget and Impoundment Control Act of 1974 (or the Congressional Budget Act) established a process for setting and employing a national budget—a roadmap of government spending for that fiscal year (the accounting period which runs from October 1 to September 30 of the next calendar year). Before then, the president had more control over the federal budget, which led to a lot of conflict with Congress—the branch that controls the purse strings according to the Constitution. That conflict became unsurmountable when President Nixon threatened to withhold appropriations in 1974, and the Congressional Budget Act was born.

This Act returned primary responsibility for the budget to Congress, though the president still had significant input. The Act removed impoundment (withholding) from the president's powers; it also created a formal process with specific procedures for developing

Congressional budgetary priorities and made it easier to reconcile differences.

The President's Annual Budget

Each year, the president submits a budget proposal to Congress for the upcoming fiscal year that highlights their policy aims and preferences. Congress does not have to honor the budget, but it makes substantial changes to the proposal while still making sure it includes enough of the president's requests to avoid disharmony between the branches. After all, Congress does need the president to sign off on legislation, so it rarely disregards the budget proposal entirely.

MANDATORY AND DISCRETIONARY SPENDING

There are two main categories of federal government spending: mandatory and discretionary. The bulk of the annual budget comes from mandatory spending, and it doesn't require a vote from Congress. Discretionary spending needs to be appropriated (designated and approved) by Congress.

Mandatory spending, also called direct spending, comes from existing law. Examples include Social Security and Medicare benefits. Since these expenditures are already authorized, they must be funded every year and cannot be cut.

Discretionary spending needs to be appropriated by Congress and approved by the president every year. This money includes military, transportation, and environmental spending. This is the area of the budget where cuts can be made to help reduce the deficit. The annual appropriation bills are the ones that Congress votes on (or at least they're supposed to) to set the fiscal year budget. Once the budget gets passed, it is sent to the president, who will either sign or veto it.

Sometimes, there may also be supplemental appropriations to cover things that weren't included in the annual budget. Examples include additional spending during the COVID-19 crisis, where Congress appropriated funds for test kits, expanded unemployment benefits, and economic impact payments.

One major budget item doesn't quite fit into either of those categories: interest. The United States has more than $34 trillion in debt, a mind-boggling number. The interest payments on that came to $357 billion for the 2023 fiscal year alone. While many policymakers and economists hold the interest in a separate category, it's technically considered a mandatory expenditure because not paying it could make further borrowing impossible, therefore crippling the US economy.

BUDGET RECONCILIATION

When Congress can't agree on and pass a budget, the ruling party can turn to a process called budget reconciliation. Unlike the typical sixty votes to pass a bill in the Senate, the reconciliation rules call for a simple majority in both chambers. This means that a reconciliation bill can't get held up by a filibuster in the Senate. Senators are allowed no more than twenty hours to debate the bill before voting.

This process was designed to help Congress pass budgets (now, it's also used on other types of legislative issues). To make sure Congress doesn't overuse this power, reconciliation comes with some special, limiting rules. For example, it's only supposed to be used once a year and only on budget issues.

Reconciliation—also known as the Byrd rule, named after Robert Byrd, the senator primarily responsible for writing it—can only be used for things that change the amount of money that the federal government is spending or bringing in. Its intent is to streamline the process for enacting budget-related bills, such as new tax acts, with a simple majority vote. It also specifically excludes certain things from reconciliation like Social Security, items that have a miniscule effect on the budget, and things that would increase the deficit after ten years.

Since budget reconciliation was introduced in 1974, Congress has used it almost thirty times, and twenty-two of those acts have been turned into law. Both parties have relied on this rule to advance legislation that would otherwise have stalled.

WHERE YOUR MONEY ACTUALLY WENT

In June 2024, the federal government had already spent around $4.49 trillion for fiscal year 2024. This figure, taken from the US Treasury, includes $576 billion on national defense, $595 billion on healthcare (Medicaid, the Centers for Disease Control and Prevention, and more), $601 billion on interest, and $475 billion on income security (nutrition and housing assistance, military retirement, and unemployment). Plus, there's $141 billion spent on education, training, employment, and social services; $70 billion on community and regional development; $82 billion on transportation; and $162 billion on "other" (which includes such things as disaster relief and renewable energy).

The largest fiscal expenditure is Social Security, but that doesn't work the same way as the other budget items. Funding for Social

Security comes strictly from Social Security tax revenues, not from income taxes.

SOME OF THE UNCONVENTIONAL WAYS TO USE TAX DOLLARS

The majority of your tax dollars go toward services that seem reasonable, like the military and healthcare, but some of it is spent on things you'd never imagine. Some of them may make you laugh, while others will make you mad. While none of these expenses comes close to the billions of dollars spent on big-ticket budget items, added up they could make a significant difference for many underfunded programs. Some unconventional uses of taxpayer dollars over the past ten years include: subsidies running to over $10 million for huge agricultural corporations to help support their farming efforts; a National Institutes of Health grant for over $700,000 to study the effects of nicotine addiction on zebra fish; and lastly a study showing that fraternity members drink more (on average) than other college students, based on a $5 million grant from the National Institute on Alcohol Abuse and Alcoholism.

If you take a closer look at federal spending for any year, you'll find things like these tucked inside. Each expenditure comes with justifications, but that probably won't make them feel any more acceptable.

Chapter 2

The US Tax Code

The United States tax code is messy, voluminous, and completely overwhelming, even for seasoned tax professionals. This overly complicated system can make it difficult for Americans to understand how much they're supposed to pay every year. It's so convoluted that entering the exact same information into different tax software programs can yield different results, and different tax professionals working with the same data can also come up with varying results. Even weirder: More than one of them can be technically correct.

How did it get this way? It all starts with Congress, the body responsible for creating the tax laws that become part of the Internal Revenue Code (IRC). The IRS then has to interpret, apply, and enforce those laws. Seems straightforward but mix in presidents and political agendas that change all the time, and you can start to see how this system got out of control.

CONGRESS CREATES TAX LAW

Representation Votes for Taxation

Though it's common to blame the IRS for convoluted, cryptic, and unfair tax rules, it's actually Congress (and only Congress) that writes and passes all the federal tax laws in the United States. Those laws collectively make up the Internal Revenue Code, which is thousands of pages long.

The main purpose of tax laws is to generate revenue for the country, a large portion of the income side of the federal budget. But Congress also uses the tax code to incentivize and disincentivize all sorts of actions, and the tax code also influences public behaviors. That's why the tax code is so long, convoluted, and confusing. And it all starts in Congress with formal tax legislation.

HOW A TAX BILL BECOMES A LAW

All tax bills get their start in the House of Representatives. That's because the House represents individual citizens, while the Senate technically represents the states. Each bill goes through the same basic series of steps, which can last anywhere from days to months to years, taking longer during more contentious Congressional sessions.

1. A member (or members) of the House creates a tax bill, often referred to as sponsoring a bill.
2. The bill gets sent to the House Ways and Means Committee, which is responsible for raising revenue to fund the federal

government; its members debate the merits and then write the proposed tax bill.

3. The Committee sends their bill to the House as a whole, where it gets debated, marked up (edited), and amended.
4. The House votes on the bill.
5. If the bill passes by a simple majority, it gets sent on to the Senate. If it does not pass, the bill dies.
6. The Senate Committee on Finance reviews the bill and usually rewrites it.
7. The new Finance Committee version of the bill goes to the Senate floor to be voted on.
8. Once this bill passes the Senate, it generally goes to the Joint Committee on Taxation (JCT), which is made up of both representatives and senators, so they can come up with a compromise version of the bill.
9. The new compromise version of the bill is sent back to both chambers of Congress for a vote.
10. Once both chambers pass the bill, it gets sent to the president for either approval or veto.

When the president accepts and signs the bill into law, it gets handed over to the appropriate agencies—the Treasury Department and the IRS for tax laws—so they can carry out its provisions. In the case of tax law, this can involve figuring out the logistics of how to interpret and implement all of the provisions in the new law.

If the president vetoes the bill, it gets sent back to the House along with an explanation of why and what it would take for the president to accept it. Congress can then make those changes and send it back to the president for their signature, or Congress may override the president's veto with a two-thirds majority vote in each chamber.

THE JOINT COMMITTEE ON TAXATION (JCT)

Originally created in 1926 as part of that year's Revenue Act, the JCT is a nonpartisan congressional group that helps both the House and the Senate fulfill their tax legislation duties. The JCT staff includes highly specialized professionals—tax lawyers, accountants, economists, statisticians, information technology specialists, and administrators. The committee is intimately involved with every step in the tax legislation process, including:

- Preparing pamphlets for the House Ways and Means Committee and the Senate Finance Committee hearings on tax legislation proposals. The pamphlets typically include detailed economic and legal analyses of the topics being discussed, as well as an overview of the issues.
- Conducting studies to help determine the short- and long-term social and economic effects of tax legislation proposals.
- Assisting in writing tax legislation bills, including proposals that may end up as part of larger tax bills. The JCT helps draft the legal language and create descriptions of what's included in each proposal.
- Figuring out how much tax revenue a proposal is projected to generate, which is called a revenue estimate. Those revenue estimates must (by law) be used as the official estimates for any tax legislation making its way through Congress.
- Creating compromise versions of tax bills when the House and Senate versions differ to reconcile those differences.

The JCT serves the vital function of ensuring continuity throughout the tax legislation process to avoid costly delays and offer objective, fact-based perspectives. They make sure that the proposed laws are feasible (at least from an administrative perspective) so that the IRS can carry them out effectively.

LOBBYISTS GET INVOLVED

Lobbyists are people who work for organizations and private interest groups with the goal of influencing legislation in these groups' favor. These professionals aim to sway politicians' opinions so they'll take action that will benefit the people, businesses, or other groups that the lobbyists represent. Lobbyists have access to lawmakers that most citizens don't, and that gives them the inside track for shaping legislation.

Lobbying organizations that work with the federal government have to report that to Congress and to the IRS by filling out special forms that specify which issues they support. The IRS disclosure is primarily because lobbyists are prohibited from using a tax-exempt status. In addition, some of their expenses are nondeductible, even if they would normally be if claimed by a different type of organization.

As of 2023, there were more than 12,500 active lobbyists overall working to influence federal legislators, spending around $4.2 billion. The income tax return preparation industry—think H&R Block and TurboTax—relies heavily on lobbyists to steer toward rules that support their paid products and away from free filing, for example. Overhauling the tax code, keeping corporate tax rates low, and pushing for specific deductions (like interest expense and depreciation) are among their top targets.

THE INTERNAL REVENUE CODE (IRC) AND THE IRS

Enter the Labyrinth

When Congress passes new tax laws, they become enshrined in the Internal Revenue Code (IRC) to be interpreted and administered by the IRS. Both of these can strike fear in the hearts of most Americans: The IRC is confusing and impossible to get right, and the IRS could come after you and seize your assets.

While all of that is technically true, they don't work like that, practically speaking. Yes, the tax code is complex, but unless you have a complicated tax situation, that probably won't affect you (if you do, you should work with a tax professional). The IRS can take steps—like asset seizure or wage garnishment—to settle tax debts, but only if you owe them money and don't make any attempts to pay. The IRS wants you to get it right, even though it doesn't seem that way.

BREAKING DOWN THE IRC

The IRC is broken down into eleven sections called subtitles. Each subtitle is further broken down into chapters, subchapters, parts, subparts, sections, subsections, paragraphs, subparagraphs, clauses, and subclauses. The numbering system can get confusing at first, but it's indexed to help people find the specific piece of information they're looking for among the thousands of numbered sections. The sections don't start renumbering as you pass through different subtitles. For example, Subtitle B contains sections 2001 to 2704.

Typically, people (mainly lawyers and tax professionals) will cite sections using the IRC numbering scheme, which uses capital and lowercase letters, numbers, and Roman numerals to differentiate sections from paragraphs and paragraphs from clauses. When citing code, professionals refer to the section number. For example, IRC §74(c) discusses taxable prizes and awards.

THE IRC COVERS EVERYTHING

Any kind of income you can think of—and even some that you wouldn't—are included in the IRC. No matter how you gain money or assets, the federal government taxes it. Some of the taxable items most people are surprised by include babysitting money, bribes, kickbacks, office pool prizes, fantasy football winnings, drug dealings, cryptocurrencies, criminal activities that generate income, raffle prizes, and found property.

The Paperless Initiative

The IRS launched a paperless initiative to cut down on processing backlogs in 2024. To that end, they've begun allowing more tax and non-tax forms (like requests for information) to be e-filed and will allow digital responses to IRS notices and correspondence. According to the agency, approximately 94% of taxpayers won't ever need to send paper mail to the IRS. These upgrades come courtesy of the Inflation Reduction Act.

You may have noticed that some of these are illegal activities. Under the IRC, criminal dealings that result in profits count as taxable self-employment income. And they expect you to report that income and pay the taxes, just like everyone else.

A BRIEF HISTORY OF THE IRS

The Office of the Commissioner of Internal Revenue, the earliest version of the IRS, was created by President Lincoln in 1862 to help collect the nation's first income taxes. Though that tax would be repealed just ten years later, the office lingered. When the Wilson Tariff Act restored income taxes in 1894, it created an income tax division inside the Bureau of Internal Revenue. That version lasted only a year before it was disbanded and the income tax repealed again.

Flash forward to 1913 when the Sixteenth Amendment became an official part of the Constitution, breathing new life into the Bureau of Internal Revenue. The Bureau created the Personal Income Tax Division and Correspondence Unit to help deal with the mountain of questions they were receiving about the new tax laws.

In 1919, to help the federal government deal with an unmanageable criminal contingent, the Bureau's powers were expanded to administer The National Prohibition Enforcement Act. To accomplish this, they brought on hundreds of new, highly trained agents to uncover bootlegging schemes and corruption.

The Bureau was tasked with collecting Social Security taxes once that law was enacted in 1935, along with developing the precursor to withholding taxes. With so much to administer, they began to modernize in 1948 with new technologies like punch cards and electric typewriters, and finally computers in 1950.

The Bureau underwent a comprehensive overhaul in 1953 and was officially renamed the Internal Revenue Service. The new focus was largely about customer—meaning taxpayer—outreach and education. By the early 1960s, another computer revolution hit the IRS when they launched an automated data processing system. As technology advanced, the IRS embraced it, always striving to process tax returns more quickly and accurately. Electronic filing with IRS e-file hit the scene in 1991, with the agency finding that more than 90% of household returns used the system for 2023 returns.

The IRS Restructuring and Reform Act of 1998 brought huge changes to the agency, reorganizing to more closely resemble the private sector. Four primary divisions were created, each focusing on a specific type of taxpayer needs. These divisions are Wage and Investment, Small Business/Self-Employed, Large and Mid-Size Business, and Tax Exempt and Government Entities.

The agency also added more digital tools for taxpayers including a withholding calculator, a "Where's My Refund?" resource, and the Free File system.

WHO WORKS AT THE IRS?

Contrary to what many people think, the IRS isn't staffed solely by armed auditors. With a staff of over 90,000 and plans to increase to 105,000 by fiscal year 2025, the agency does much more than examine tax returns. The agency staff has many other functions in addition to conducting audits, including:

- Helping people get tax documents, make changes to their accounts, and set up payment plans at Taxpayer Assistance Centers (TACs)
- Designing and operating accounting systems
- Creating, customizing, and debugging apps and software
- Planning research initiatives to revise tax administration policies and practices

- Investigating criminal violations of the IRC, led by the Criminal Investigation division
- Providing regulations and revenue rulings to help taxpayers understand and comply with tax law

Of the total employees at the IRS, approximately 40% work in enforcement and 44.8% focus on customer service. The agency is led by the commissioner, currently (as of May 2024) Daniel Werfel, who is the fiftieth person to hold that position.

IRS AUDITS

When people think about the IRS, their minds usually jump to fear about getting audited. While you've probably heard audit horror stories about property being seized and people going to jail, that hardly ever happens. In fact, most audits actually take place by mail, with the IRS explaining why they disagree with your tax return and proposing what they think you should pay instead.

Every year, the IRS conducts both random and targeted audits, but targeted is not as scary as it sounds. In most cases, these audits are due to mismatches caught by the computer system—for example, if the salary you reported doesn't match your W2 or you left out some interest income by mistake. A much smaller proportion of targeted audits occur because something on your tax return doesn't make sense, like if your income is $60,000 and you had $40,000 of charitable donations, or some of your business expenses seemed out of whack compared to your revenues and compared to similar businesses. Overall, the IRS audits only around 0.38% of tax returns, so your odds are pretty good.

HOW THE TAX CODE WORKS

Taxes in Ten Million Words

The Internal Revenue Code is the United States tax code administered by the IRS. It includes thousands of numbered sections, and each of those contain definitions and detailed rules of how to apply each section in specific circumstances. These legal requirements are all contained in Title 26 of the Code of Federal Regulations, also known as 26 CFR.

The IRC is extensive and gets down into the smallest details of taxpayer responsibilities. It covers everything from tax filing due dates to instructions for forms and schedules to how to manage a dispute.

READ THE SUBTITLES

Each IRC subtitle contains the down and dirty details for that portion of the IRC code. The eleven main subtitles include:

- Subtitle A: Income Taxes
- Subtitle B: Estate and Gift Taxes (sections 2001–2704)
- Subtitle C: Employment Taxes (sections 3101–3512)
- Subtitle D: Miscellaneous Excise Taxes (sections 4041–4982)
- Subtitle E: Alcohol, Tobacco, and Certain Other Excise Taxes (sections 5001–5872)
- Subtitle F: Procedure and Administration (sections 6012–7874)
- Subtitle G: Joint Committee on Taxation (sections 8001–8023)
- Subtitle H: Financing of Presidential Election Campaigns (sections 9001–9042)

- Subtitle I: Trust Fund Code (sections 9500–9602)
- Subtitle J: Coal Industry Health Benefits (sections 9702–9722)
- Subtitle K: Group Health Plan Requirements (sections 9801–9834)

Most people will be concerned with the contents of Subtitle A, and many business owners will also need some familiarity with Subtitle C.

Subtitle A has six chapters, but most people will only be affected by Chapter 1: Normal Taxes and Surtaxes, and Chapter 2: Tax on Self-Employment Income. Chapter 1 has twenty-six subchapters that detail everything from computing taxable income (subchapter B) to capital gains and losses (subchapter P) to S corporation taxation (subchapter S). Each of these components gets broken down further and further until you get down to the actual language of the law.

HOW BIG IS IT?

The IRC is unbearably long and complicated. The Government Printing Office sells a physical book version that comes in a minimum of two volumes (you can buy smaller sections too), and together they run around 2,600 pages. You can find the complete Title 26 on the House website at https://uscode.house.gov. However, keep in mind that this is just the code itself, and no tax accountant or lawyer relies on the literal letter of the law alone.

The IRC is where tax law starts—the legislation Congress wants enacted. To make the laws usable, the IRS creates regulations (also called tax regulations or Treasury regulations) and other clarifications to implement them. They give instructions on how to comply with the law correctly. For example, they detail things like how people must take required minimum distributions from retirement plans or guidelines for what makes someone a qualifying child. These regulations are about three times longer than the IRC itself. You can find the complete tax regulations on the Code of Federal Regulations website at www.ecfr.gov.

Unfortunately, understanding tax law doesn't stop there. In addition to the laws and regulations, there's a huge body of case law and court decisions. When taxpayers disagree with IRS determinations, they can take their cases to the United States Tax Court. The Court's decisions become part of the overall tax code, setting official precedents for how taxpayers should proceed in similar circumstances. This is the most extensive portion of the code, and it can provide specific guidance for tax questions.

REGULATIONS

When Congress enacts new tax laws, the IRS has to figure out how to apply them. That includes understanding and interpreting the new laws, then translating that understanding into manageable procedures and processes. The agency does this by issuing regulations, or guidance for how the law will actually work. Those regulations start out as proposals published as a Notice of Proposed Rulemaking (NPRM). The public has time to comment on the proposals, generally through written comments, though sometimes public hearings are held. After all input has been considered, the final regulation is published in the Federal Register as a Treasury Decision (TD).

The point of the regulations is to make compliance clear for taxpayers and tax professionals. It doesn't always work out that way, leading to further interpretation and even sometimes altering the way the statute will be applied going forward.

REVENUE RULINGS

The IRS publishes revenue rulings in the Internal Revenue Bulletin (IRB) to detail their interpretation of particular tax laws. While these rulings don't have the same legal strength as the tax laws themselves, and they're not binding in court, they can be used as precedents (examples of acceptable actions) for taxpayers dealing with the IRS.

Revenue rulings deal with specific facts rather than theoretical situations. The IRS decides how the laws apply to a fact pattern, and then other taxpayers can rely on that viewpoint in similar circumstances. If a taxpayer ignores the requirements or tax treatment published in a revenue ruling, they may be subject to additional taxes, tax penalties, or other IRS actions.

You can find a complete history of revenue rulings on the IRS website (www.irs.gov) in the IRB section. Rulings are numbered based on the year that they're issued, so revenue rulings decided in 2024 would start with 2024–##, for example.

Private Letter Rulings

When a taxpayer is unsure of the tax treatment for unusual or complex circumstances, they can ask the IRS for guidance in the form of a private letter ruling (PLR). The taxpayer provides the facts and requests that the IRS advise them on the proper tax treatment ahead of time. PLRs apply only to that taxpayer at that time unless the IRS decides to expand it to a revenue ruling. Unfortunately, PLRs can be revoked or revised at any time if the agency determines that the ruling was wrong or doesn't mesh with current policy.

CASE LAW

When taxpayers disagree with IRS determinations, they can take their cases to the United States Tax Court, an independent judiciary body that settles tax disputes. Based in Washington, DC, the Tax Court has judges that preside in seventy-four cities across the US for federal tax issues. Tax Court cases generally involve taxpayers who have received a notification from the IRS that they owe money. When the taxpayer thinks the IRS is wrong, they can file a petition with the Tax Court, which stops the collections process until the case is decided.

Many of these cases settle before going to trial. When there is a full trial, the judge will issue their findings in their decision. There are three types of decisions:

1. Summary decisions, issued in expedited procedures for small tax cases where the taxpayer owes less than $50,000. These decisions can't be appealed or used as precedents.
2. Regular decisions that involve cases with unusual or new points of tax law and are decided by a panel of judges. These decisions are recorded publicly and published in the *United States Tax Court Reports*.
3. Memorandum decisions, for regular tax cases that don't involve unusual or new points but seek to clarify settled law by interpreting specific facts. These decisions are published unofficially in *Tax Court Memorandum Decisions*.

Regular decisions are considered the strongest authority and can be used as precedent. You can find Tax Court decisions and orders on the United States Tax Court website at www.ustaxcourt.gov.

TAX VOCABULARY

From "AGI" to "Schedule Z"

Tax law includes a lot of lingo and concepts that can be difficult for taxpayers to fully grasp. Even tax professionals, who normally take annual classes about tax law, still often need help. Understanding the lingo of the tax world is an important part of getting a handle on your personal tax situation. You don't need to know the entire tax code inside and out—hardly anyone does—but knowing some basic tax vocabulary will come in handy when you're trying to figure out your taxes.

PHASE OUTS

Many tax benefits get phased out (incrementally reduced to zero) based on the person's income level, specifically their adjusted gross income or modified adjusted gross income (more on that in a moment). The goal of phase outs is to limit tax advantages for high earners, steering the tax benefits toward lower-income taxpayers.

The structure and calculation of phase outs differ depending on the object: whether it's a tax credit, tax deduction, or other tax-related amount. Phase outs that apply to tax credits impact all taxpayers equally (dollar-wise), while the effects of phase outs that apply to tax deductions depend on the taxpayer's marginal tax rate. Phase outs affect whether you can deduct an IRA contribution, contribute to a Roth IRA, or take full advantage of tax credits (like the Saver's Credit and the American Opportunity Tax Credit).

Unfortunately, the intent of the phase outs can sometimes backfire. For example, earning just $1 more than the upper limit of a phase out can block a taxpayer from being able to claim the Earned Income Tax Credit (EITC) or the Child Tax Credit. Losing those substantial tax benefits can be quite costly and may encourage people to limit their income so they don't end up paying thousands more in taxes.

ABOVE-THE-LINE DEDUCTIONS

Above-the-line deductions, officially called "adjustments to income" on your tax form, can be more valuable than other kinds of tax deductions. These deductions are named this way because they used to fall above the fold on paper tax returns, and these subtract from your total income (also called gross income) to come up with your adjusted gross income (AGI). Above-the-line deductions reduce your AGI, which can have a positive effect on your overall tax liability. Some of the common above-the-line deductions include:

- Traditional individual retirement account (IRA) contributions
- Contributions to health savings accounts (HSAs)
- Student loan interest
- Self-employed health insurance premiums

You can take these deductions in addition to either the standard deduction or itemized deductions on your tax return.

ADJUSTED GROSS INCOME

Adjusted gross income, or AGI, is a crucial tax calculation that's used as the starting point for many other tax calculations and phase outs. It determines which deductions and credits you might be eligible to take (or take a portion of), such as the Child Tax Credit. It also determines how much (if any) of your medical expenses can be deducted—only medical expenses in excess of 7.5% of AGI can be taken as itemized deductions. AGI also determines whether or not you can contribute to a Roth IRA.

To calculate AGI, you start with your total income from every source: W2 earnings, interest, dividends, capital gains, distributions from retirement accounts, and so on. Then you subtract "adjustments to income" (above-the-line deductions), such as educator expenses or a portion of self-employment taxes.

BRACKETS

Tax brackets seem confusing to many taxpayers, but they're really just income buckets used to figure out your total tax bill. Every dollar you earn falls into a bucket. When your income fills up the first bucket, every dollar you earn after that falls into the next bucket until that one gets filled. That cycle keeps going until you reach the overflow bucket—the top tax bracket.

In practical terms, tax brackets work like this: Let's say you're single and your taxable income came to $88,000. Based on 2024 tax brackets, you'd pay 10% on the first $11,600 of your earnings, then 12% on the next $35,550, and then 22% on the remaining $40,850. You're in the 22% tax bracket, but not all your income gets taxed at that rate, only the portion that lands in that bucket.

The last, highest rate applied to a taxpayer's income is called their marginal tax rate (in the previous example, it would be 22%). This marginal tax rate is the rate that will apply to the last dollar of taxable income.

DEPRECIATION

"Depreciation" is one of the most commonly misunderstood tax terms. Depreciation is an accounting expense designed to write off the cost of an income-producing asset (something owned like a truck, building, or computer) over time. Income-producing assets include things like machinery, equipment, and vehicles used for a business and rental properties.

The point of depreciation is to divide the cost of the asset up and expense it over its entire useful life, so it matches up with the associated revenue. For example, if you have a freelance writing business and buy a new laptop, you expect that laptop to last you for at least a few years. Depreciation is the accounting method of splitting the cost of the laptop over that whole period of time. It's a cash-free expense that helps reduce taxable income, which also reduces taxes.

Managing MACRS

The IRS dictates everything about the MACRS depreciation method, from which assets are eligible to the length of their useful lives. For example, tractors and racehorses get depreciated over three years, while breeding cattle and computers get depreciated over five years.

There are a few methods for calculating depreciation, including straight-line and accelerated. Straight-line is the most straightforward option, where you simply divide the full cost of an asset by its useful life and then expense that amount every year. For example, a $3,000 computer with a three-year useful life would result in $1,000 of depreciation expense annually. Accelerated depreciation methods use IRS tables for tax purposes, such as the accelerated cost recovery system (ACRS) and the modified accelerated cost recovery system (MACRS) tables that provide percentages to apply to the asset every year. These percentages front-load depreciation, with higher amounts than straight-line occurring in the early years that decline over time. You can find tax depreciation tables on the IRS website at www.irs.gov.

BASIS

One of the most important and complicated tax concepts, basis, affects you any time you sell an asset (like a stock or your house). Basis starts with however much you paid for the asset to acquire it. That includes the actual purchase price along with other potential acquisition costs (depending on the type of asset) like sales tax, shipping, commissions, and transfer fees.

For physical assets like real estate, basis can be adjusted if you spend money to make substantial improvements to the property. Any changes that are anticipated to last longer than a year and increase the value of the property can affect basis—for example, adding a room on to a house, rewiring an entire building, or installing a new roof can impact basis.

WHAT'S BEHIND TAX RULES?

Whose Idea Was That?

The United States tax code is unwieldy (at best), and a lot of it seems random, but every policy has some kind of reasoning behind it. Along with the general aim of raising revenue for the federal government, many tax laws were designed to dissuade or incentivize specific actions, provide benefits to a specific group of taxpayers, or quietly initiate policies that can't be legislated for some reason.

LUXURY TAXES

Luxury taxes work like sales or excise taxes that are only charged on non-essential items that typically only wealthy people buy. It may be imposed on the full cost of the product or on a portion of it, such as an extra surcharge on cars that cost more than $100,000. It's basically a "tax the rich" kind of tax, and it usually doesn't survive lobbying efforts.

Back in 1991, Congress enacted a luxury tax commonly called the yacht tax, even though it covered more than yachts. It was a 10% excise tax charged on the first retail purchases of specific goods over certain thresholds including private boats over $100,000; automobiles over $30,000; private aircraft over $250,000; jewelry over $10,000; and furs over $10,000.

The yacht industry protested heavily, claiming that this tax was costing American jobs. So President Clinton and Congress repealed this tax in 1993. Although no federal luxury taxes have been imposed since, some states do still have them in place.

SIN TAXES

Sin taxes are targeted excise taxes imposed on goods or services that are considered harmful in some way. These taxes are levied on the buyers at the time of sale. They've been in place in America since its earliest days. Common items that have been subject to sin taxes include cigarettes or other tobacco products, alcohol, candy, vaping, and gambling.

The aim of these taxes is to increase the price of items the government wants to discourage people from buying, while at the same time boosting tax revenues. Supporters of these sin taxes claim they help offset the cost of the purchases to society, such as higher healthcare expenses for smokers that drive up the costs of medical care or insurance for everyone.

GASOLINE TAXES

Americans pay excise taxes on every gallon of fuel they buy: 18.40 cents per gallon on gasoline and 24.40 cents for diesel. Those rates have been in place, unchanged, since 1993. However, they slowly climbed to this taxed rate starting in the mid-1900s.

Gasoline taxes were first introduced in 1932 in that year's Revenue Act, and they had the purpose of reducing the federal deficit. That temporary gasoline tax added one cent to the cost of every gallon. It was increased to 1.5 cents in 1940 to help the country get ready to enter World War II and stayed at that level until 1951. It was then increased up to two cents per gallon to fund the Korean War.

A shift came in 1956 when Congress created the Highway Trust Fund. The gas tax was bumped up to three cents a gallon, and every cent of revenue was pledged to build and maintain the US interstate highway system. In 1983, the rate was increased to nine cents a gallon, with a portion diverted to support mass transit.

In 1990, gas tax revenues were split: a portion remained dedicated to highways, and the rest would help reduce the federal deficit. At that time, the tax climbed to fourteen cents per gallon. A few years later, in 1993, Congress raised it again to address the deficit, bringing the total up to 18.30 cents per gallon, with another 0.1 cent per gallon tacked on to address leaking underground storage tanks.

GREEN TAX CREDITS

Clean energy tax credits, also known as green tax credits, aim to promote the purchase and use of cleaner alternatives for power production and energy efficient options. The Inflation Reduction Act expanded green credits for 2023 through 2032, with some reduced credits available in 2033 and 2034. Some green credits are geared toward businesses, but many of these potentially valuable tax credits are targeted to individual taxpayers.

The Energy Efficient Home Improvement Credit, for example, offers a tax credit of 30% of the cost (up to an annual maximum) to install qualifying certified energy efficient items such as exterior doors, windows, and skylights; furnaces, hot water heaters, and heat pumps; and home energy audits.

The Residential Clean Energy Credit offers a 30% credit (through at least 2032, then the percentage decreases) to help homeowners cover the costs of solar, wind, and geothermal power generation. It includes things like solar panels, solar-powered water heaters, wind turbines, and geothermal heat pumps.

There are also clean vehicle tax credits of up to $7,500 for taxpayers who buy new, qualified plug-in electric vehicles or fuel cell electric vehicles. You can find qualifying vehicles by going to www.fueleconomy.gov.

Lobbyists Like It Complicated

The tax prep lobby is large and powerful, and it's in their best interest to keep the tax code complex and tax filing not free. The big companies (like Intuit and H&R Block) spent more than $90 million lobbying against the IRS Free File program, and tens of millions more fighting against tax code simplification.

ENCOURAGING TAXPAYERS TO SAVE

The federal government offers several incentives to encourage people to save for retirement. Tax-advantaged retirement accounts can provide both current and future tax benefits. Individual retirement accounts (IRAs) give taxpayers a tax break for their contributions and offer tax-deferred growth (so there's no tax on earnings every year) to help those accounts build up into nest eggs. The taxes get paid later on, in retirement, when the taxpayer starts taking withdrawals. Roth IRAs don't give taxpayers a current tax benefit (they're funded with after-tax dollars) but do offer tax-free growth and tax-free withdrawals in retirement.

There are also tax benefits for employers who offer workplace retirement plans and the employees who participate in them. The most popular of these are 401(k) plans, which work like IRAs when it comes to taxes.

Lower-income taxpayers who contribute to any kind of qualified retirement plan may be eligible for the Saver's Credit worth up to $1,000 for single taxpayers or $2,000 for married couples. Depending on your income, the credit is calculated as 50%, 20%, or 10% of the first $2,000 of your retirement plan contribution ($4,000 for married couples).

BIG CHANGES WITH NEW PRESIDENTS

Putting Their Own Stamp on Things

Newly elected presidents start their terms with fresh ideas and big plans, many of them at least tangentially involving tax legislation. After all, taxes will fund their programs and initiatives and can be used as tools to influence personal and corporate actions. Sometimes the proposed changes to tax law are sweeping, while others are barely noticeable.

Although Congress is responsible for crafting and passing tax legislation, presidents can still exert influence on the direction that legislation takes. That's why big tax initiatives are usually tagged with the name of the president who signed them into law, rather than the members of Congress who actually wrote them. New presidents often have big ideas about changes they'd like to see in the tax code, and they may campaign with promises to change the tax code in favor of their main supporters.

PRESIDENT REAGAN

Reaganomics, also called trickle-down or supply-side, brought a seismic change to the US tax code. President Ronald Reagan had a new economic vision for the US based on the trickle-down theory (or supply-side economics) that included extensive tax cuts along with massive spending changes and market deregulation. The main idea was that by decreasing taxes, particularly for large corporations, you could spur economic growth, which would trickle down to the general public.

Two major pieces of tax legislation were passed while President Reagan was in office. The first was the Economic Recovery Tax Act (ERTA) of 1981, which introduced huge tax cuts. The notable takeaway here was that the top tax rate was lowered to 50% from 70%, a massive boon to the highest earners. ERTA also reduced marginal tax rates at all levels by 23%, phased in over three years.

The Tax Reform Act of 1986 lowered the top tax rate again, from 50% down to 28%, and simultaneously increased the bottom tax rate from 11% to 15%. Other provisions included:

- Mandating that long-term capital gains be taxed as ordinary income, effectively increasing the maximum capital gains rate to 28% from 20%
- Requiring Social Security numbers for all children declared as dependents on a tax return
- Expanding the alternative minimum tax (AMT)
- Increasing personal exemptions
- Increasing the home mortgage interest deduction
- Reducing the corporate tax rate to 35% from 50%
- Putting more restrictions on certain business tax deductions

The Reagan tax cuts did have some positive short-term effects on the economy, including lower inflation, reduced unemployment, and higher stock prices, which all helped with recession recovery. However, these tax policies jump-started a widening wealth gap between the very rich and everyone else, as well as increasing both the national debt and the federal deficit.

PRESIDENT CLINTON

In 1993, the 103rd Congress passed President Bill Clinton's Tax Reform Act. The driving force for this legislation was a desire to reduce the federal deficit by raising taxes and reducing spending. With this law in place, the federal budget was balanced for the first time in nearly twenty-five years, and by 1998, it produced a surplus for the first time in decades.

This tax law created two tax brackets, bringing the top income tax rates up to 36% and 39.6% while limiting itemized deductions. It removed the Medicare wage cap, meaning that tax would apply to all wages. Gasoline taxes were increased, along with taxes on Social Security benefits. On the business side, the tax deduction for business meals was decreased to 50%, and the deduction for entertainment expenses was eliminated. Unusually, this tax law worked retroactively, applying to income from the beginning of the year rather than starting the next year.

Taxpayer Relief Act of 1997

Another Clinton-era tax bill, the Taxpayer Relief Act, introduced many tax-saving opportunities still in use today. Those included the Child Tax Credit, the Lifetime Learning Credit, the Hope Credit (now called the American Opportunity Tax Credit), and the Roth IRA.

PRESIDENT BUSH

President George W. Bush brought two rounds of temporary tax cuts, first in 2001 for individual taxpayers and then in 2003 with a business focus. These cuts were supposed to expire in 2010 and 2008, but after the 2008 recession they were extended to 2012.

The Economic Growth and Tax Relief Reconciliation Act (EGTRRA) of 2001 sought to help spark economic growth following recession and brought significant tax benefits including:

- Creating the 10% income tax bracket and reducing the rates for all other tax brackets
- Increasing the Child Tax Credit to $1,000 (up from $500) per qualifying child
- Doubling the standard deduction for married couples filing jointly, effectively eliminating the "marriage penalty"
- Raising the age for required minimum distributions (RMDs) from retirement accounts
- Creating "catch-up" contributions for employees over age fifty so they could make extra contributions to retirement plans
- Getting rid of the time limit for student loan interest tax deductions
- Reducing the maximum gift and estate tax to 50% (down from 55%), with additional annual decreases

Two years later, the Jobs and Growth Tax Relief Reconciliation Act (JGTRRA) added more tax cuts into the mix. These mainly focused on the business community, though pieces did address personal tax issues. Highlights of JGTRRA included reduced taxes on long-term capital gains and qualified dividends, sped-up EGTRRA tax cuts, and substantially increased small business tax deductions.

These two tax laws helped move the country out of recession, increased investment in the stock market, and spurred economic growth. At the same time they led to decreased tax revenues, an increase in the national debt, and a larger federal budget deficit.

NEW PRESIDENTS REWRITE THE RULES

Let's Do the Opposite

Presidents like to put their own stamp on tax law, often choosing to undo the work of their predecessors. When Congress is on their side, the president's plan can slide smoothly through. When it's not, Congressional resistance may lead to more compromise from the president's team to get their pet projects on the slate.

The most recent Oval Office inhabitants all brought on big tax-related changes. Some lasted through multiple presidencies, while others were quickly gutted by their successors. This flip-flopping has affected everything from health insurance to take-home pay to corporate profits. The only thing that's sure to stay the same is that the next president will want to put their mark on the US tax code.

PRESIDENT OBAMA

The tax centerpiece of the Obama Administration was the Affordable Care Act (ACA), also known as Obamacare. The goal: to provide healthcare to more Americans. It involved a combination of increased taxes and tax cuts to accomplish this healthcare coverage, introducing more than twenty new provisions to the tax code. It enabled more people to access health insurance, such as those with pre-existing conditions, and offered subsidized premiums based on income so more people could afford health insurance.

The most controversial provision was the individual mandate, a provision that required taxpayers who could afford it to purchase health insurance or pay an extra tax based on their adjusted gross income. While the individual mandate got the lion's share of attention, the ACA included many other new tax rules including:

- The employer mandate, requiring all businesses with at least fifty full-time employees to provide health insurance options
- A 3.8% net investment income tax for high earners
- A Branded Prescription Drug Fee program (for drug manufacturers selling to federal programs like Medicare and Medicaid)
- An additional Medicare tax of 0.9% on taxpayers earning more than $200,000 ($250,000 if married filing jointly)

Many provisions of the ACA, starting with the individual mandate, have since been neutralized or repealed, though the ones previously listed are still in effect.

PRESIDENT TRUMP

President Trump sparked some of the biggest changes in tax law since Ronald Reagan with the Tax Cuts and Jobs Act of 2017 (TCJA). Tax cuts for corporations were permanent, while individual tax cuts were temporary and most provisions set to expire after 2025. That expiration date allowed the bill to pass under the reconciliation rules, blocking a potential Democratic filibuster.

On the personal tax side, the TCJA substantially increased the standard deduction, got rid of personal exemptions, repealed the individual mandate (from the ACA), and lowered most income tax rates. It also increased the Child Tax Credit to $2,000 and made a portion of it refundable ($1,600 for 2024), and it created a non-refundable tax credit for dependents that aren't children (such as aging parents). Finally, it increased the estate tax exemption ($13.61 million for 2024), capped the state and local tax (SALT) deduction to $10,000, and eliminated some miscellaneous deductions such as moving expenses and union dues.

On the business side, the TCJA repealed the alternative minimum tax (AMT) for corporations and permanently set the corporate tax rate to 21%. The law also created a special 20% tax deduction for pass-through businesses, which pass their income through to the business owners to be reported on their personal tax returns.

The Setting Up Every Community for Retirement (SECURE) Act also passed during President Trump's tenure. This law made it easier for employers to offer retirement plans, included more employees in the plans, increased the age for taking RMDs to seventy-two, and authorized penalty-free early retirement withdrawals of up to $5,000 for the birth or adoption of a child.

2026 Rewind

Most of the provisions of the TCJA set to expire in 2025 will directly affect millions of taxpayers starting in 2026. For example, the standard deduction will revert to its 2017 amount of $6,350 adjusted up for inflation (compared to $14,600 for 2024), and the Child Tax Credit will go back to just $1,000 per qualifying child.

The Coronavirus Aid, Relief, and Economic Security (CARES) Act helped struggling Americans deal with the fallout of COVID-19, and it included some lifeline tax provisions—for example, direct economic impact payments, programs to subsidize payroll expenses for small businesses, and above-the-line deductions for charitable contributions. It also helped people take emergency money from retirement accounts without facing the 10% early withdrawal penalty.

PRESIDENT BIDEN

Coming in during the COVID-19 pandemic, President Biden jumped right in to take action to help the US through the crisis. Major tax legislation enacted by President Biden included (as of February 2024) the American Rescue Plan Act (ARPA) of 2021, the SECURE 2.0 Act, and the Inflation Reduction Act.

ARPA aimed to help the country through the devastating effects of COVID-19 and was one of the largest economic recovery acts ever enacted, with a price tag of $1.9 trillion. It included another round of direct stimulus payments, extended and expanded unemployment benefits, made the first $10,200 of unemployment benefits received in 2020 tax-free for many taxpayers, and further expanded the Child Tax Credit by introducing advance payments for struggling families.

The SECURE 2.0 Act focused on making it easier for Americans to save for retirement. A provision for this Act included raising the age for taking required minimum distributions (RMDs) to seventy-three in 2023, increasing to seventy-five in 2033. It also cut the penalty for failing to take proper RMDs in half to 25% down from 50%, removed the RMD requirement for participants in employer-sponsored Roth retirement plans, and increased annual workplace retirement plan catch-up contributions for people fifty and older to $10,000 extra starting in 2025.

The Inflation Reduction Act was a pared-down version of Biden's Build Back Better plan. The Act's main tax-related provisions include a 15% minimum corporate tax rate, a 1% excise tax on corporate stock buybacks, increased funding for IRS enforcement against tax cheats, extension of ACA health insurance premium subsidies through 2025, and new or updated climate-based tax incentives like the electronic vehicle tax credits. This law also protects families earning $400,000 or less per year by not imposing any new taxes on them.

Chapter 3

Different Types of Personal Taxes

If you add up all of the taxes you pay, the total is probably your single biggest annual expense. We're constantly flooded with taxes, even when we don't notice it. That's because we think of them in separate unconnected buckets, but underneath they're all taxes. The most common personal taxes we're subject to are income taxes, payroll taxes, capital gains taxes, property taxes, sales and use taxes, and gift and estate taxes.

Not everyone will have to deal with all of these, but most of us are dealing with most of them, even if sometimes indirectly. For example, if you rent your home, you don't pay property taxes directly, but they are included in your monthly rent payment.

Bottom line: If you add up all the taxes you pay, you'll be shocked by how much of your budget they take up collectively. That's why it's crucial to understand all of the different types of personal taxes and how they eat away at your money.

INCOME TAXES

A Penny Earned Is a Penny Taxed

As soon as you start earning money, you pay taxes (or at least you're supposed to). Your income was taxed the moment you received your first paycheck and you realized how much money was missing from it. But what you might not have realized is that different types of income get taxed in different ways, and not all of them are equal.

While you are required by law to pay taxes, you're not required to *over*pay. However, many people do end up overpaying because they fear the IRS and potential consequences. Evading taxes, meaning not paying what you owe, is illegal. Avoiding taxes, meaning doing everything you can to minimize your tax bill, is perfectly legal. In fact, the ability to reduce your tax liability is built into the tax system in the form of deductions and credits. Making sure you take advantage of all of the appropriate reductions in your tax bill does not increase your risk of IRS issues, but it does make sure you don't pay a penny more in taxes than you need to.

WITHHOLDING TAXES

When most people think about income taxes, they're thinking about payroll withholding, the money taken out of every paycheck that goes to the government. Though not all withholding taxes are income taxes, they usually do make up the lion's share of deductions from your paycheck. Those include federal, state, and local income taxes based on the information you included on your Form

W-4 when you were hired or made changes to it. (While Social Security and Medicare taxes are also withheld from your paycheck, they aren't technically income taxes, so they'll be discussed in a later section.)

The IRS counts withholding taxes as being paid in equal amounts all year long, even if they aren't. In fact, even if you withheld no taxes for the first six months of the year, then doubled up on withholding for the remainder, the IRS would calculate that you'd been paying into the system all year long. So if you do a recommended tax checkup in the fall and see that you've been paying in either too much or too little, you can change your withholding accordingly.

Filling Out Your W-4

All employees fill out Form W-4 (the Employee's Withholding Certificate) when they start new jobs. This form tells their employers how much money to withhold for federal income taxes, and it collects tax-related information, like your filing status and number of dependents. There are options to fill out if you have more than one job, or if you want extra money withheld. Remember to update your W-4 any time there's a significant change in your circumstances (marriage, having a child, starting a side gig).

You can also adjust your withholding to cover any income that doesn't have taxes taken out automatically, like an investment or income from a side gig. Doing this can take the burden of making estimated tax payments (more on those later) off of your plate. All it takes is an updated Form W-4 to have your employer change the amount you have withheld every pay period.

UNDERSTANDING TAX BRACKETS

Tax brackets are really just income ranges and the tax percentage applied to income in that range. As of 2024, the United States has seven tax brackets, which depend on your filing status; the brackets for single filers are different than the brackets for married couples filing jointly, for example. Each bracket has a corresponding tax rate, and all of the income in that bracket gets taxed at its rate. When your income is higher than the end range of a bracket, it moves to the next one, and that portion of income gets taxed at the new bracket's rate.

This is what the tax brackets look like for 2024:

TAX RATE	SINGLE	HEAD OF HOUSEHOLD	MARRIED FILING JOINTLY	MARRIED FILING SEPARATELY
10%	$0 – $11,600	$0 – $16,550	$0 – $23,200	$0 – $11,600
12%	$11,601 – $47,150	$16,551 – $63,100	$23,201 – $94,300	$11,601 – $47,150
22%	$47,151 – $100,525	$63,101 – $100,500	$94,301 – $201,050	$47,151 – $100,525
24%	$100,526 – $191,950	$100,501 – $191,950	$201,051 – $383,900	$100,526 – $191,950
32%	$191,951 – $243,725	$191,951 – $243,700	$383,901 – $487,450	$191,951 – $243,725
35%	$243,726 – $609,350	$243,701 – $609,350	$487,451 – $731,200	$243,726 – $365,600
37%	$609,351 and more	$609,351 and more	$731,201 and more	$365,601 and more

It's a little confusing to talk about these in theory, so let's look at an example (for 2024) with numbers. Let's say you have $65,000 of taxable income and use the single filing status. You would pay 10% tax on your first $11,600 of income, or $1,160. Then, you'd pay 12% on the next range of income ($11,601 to $47,150) which comes to $4,265.88. Finally, you'd pay 22% on the rest of your income ($47,151 to $65,000), which would equal $3,926.78. Your total tax would be $9,352.66.

Contrary to what most people think, the highest tax percent for your income only gets applied to that bracket, not to all of your income. Your true tax rate would be calculated by dividing your total tax by your taxable income. In this example, the overall tax rate (called the effective tax rate) would come to 14.38% ($9,352.66/$65,000.00).

So when does your tax bracket matter? This system affects you most when you're about to move into the next bracket, where every additional dollar you earn would get taxed at the higher rate. You can take steps to avoid that jump up by using income-lowering strategies like deferring income or accelerating deductions, for example.

ALTERNATIVE MINIMUM TAX (AMT)

Alternative minimum taxes (AMT) are among the most frustratingly complicated tax rules. Like the term implies, the AMT is the least amount a person has to pay in taxes regardless of any tax credits or deductions they'd otherwise be allowed to take. It forces income taxes to be calculated twice under two different sets of rules. Whichever amount is higher is the tax that has to be paid.

The AMT kicks in if your income exceeds specific exemption amounts: $85,700 for single filers and $133,300 for married filing jointly in 2024. The point of this is to make sure higher earners pay a fairer share of taxes (even if it doesn't actually always work that way).

The AMT uses a different set of rules to get to the amount of tax owed. Its calculations add some "tax preference" items back to

AGI for a new taxable total called the alternative minimum taxable income (AMTI). Common tax preference items include state and local tax deductions, tax-exempt interest, certain business expenses (such as accelerated depreciation), and certain investment income (such as long-term capital gains).

After the preference item add-back, you subtract the AMT exemption ($85,700 for single filers and $133,300 for married filing jointly in 2024) to figure out the final taxable amount. The AMT has just two tax rates, 26% and 28%, depending on how much your AMTI is. If this tax total comes out to more than the amount you'd owe using the regular rules, you have to pay the AMT instead.

EMPLOYMENT AND PAYROLL TAXES

Who the %$#! Is FICA?

If you earn money by working, whether it's for yourself or someone else, those earnings are subject to employment taxes. Some financial professionals include withheld income taxes in this category, but this section simply discusses the non-income taxes in this category. Technically, payroll taxes are a subset of employment taxes and usually refer to Social Security and Medicare.

All employment taxes are remitted to the IRS by employers. Some employment taxes are paid only by employers, while others are shared between employers and employees. When you own a business with employees, your company will also be responsible for some additional employer-only taxes, usually related to unemployment on the federal and state levels. The biggest chunk of employment taxes goes to the Federal Insurance Contributions Act (FICA), which includes Social Security and Medicare taxes.

SOCIAL SECURITY

Ever since January 1937, American workers have been paying into the Social Security system, which is designed to supply income to people in retirement (and to people who can't work due to disease or disability). Millions of Americans receive benefits every year, fully funded by the taxes being paid into this separate system, which is officially called the Old Age, Survivors, and Disability (OASDI) program.

Social Security taxes are 12.4% on all earned income—meaning salaries, wages, and self-employment profits—up to the cap of $168,600 (in 2024). This tax is generally split between employees and employers, with each contributing 6.2% of earnings.

In order to qualify for retirement benefits, you need to rack up a minimum of forty work credits throughout your lifetime. Your payments into this system work sort of like insurance premiums that go toward your eventual payments in retirement. That's why the amount of benefits you'll receive when you retire will be directly related to your lifetime earnings.

MEDICARE

Along with Social Security, the federal government charges all workers for Medicare (or hospital insurance) tax. These collections go toward funding Part A of the Medicare program, which covers hospital, hospice, and nursing home care for Americans over age sixty-five. The US government holds this tax money in the Hospital Insurance Trust Fund. Medicare tax is charged at a total rate of 2.9%, with employees and employers each paying half (self-employed people pay the whole amount).

Medicare tax gets applied to all your earned income, unlike Social Security tax, which comes with an annual wage cap. High earners may be subject to an additional Medicare tax of 0.9%. This applies to all of their income over the stated wage threshold limit, which is $200,000 for single filers, $250,000 for married couples filing jointly, and $125,000 for married couples filing separate returns in 2024.

FEDERAL UNEMPLOYMENT TAX

Federal Unemployment Tax (FUTA, where the "A" stands for "Act") is an employer-only employment tax that applies to non-household and non-agricultural employees. The rate is 6% on the first $7,000 of wages (called the FUTA wage base) for each employee. The collected FUTA funds are used in connection with state funds to provide unemployment compensation.

FUTA gets reported annually on IRS Form 940. It's required if in any quarter you paid at least $1,500 in wages or had at least one employee for twenty or more weeks during the year. If the employer also paid state unemployment taxes, they may get a credit for up to 5.4% against their total FUTA liability. The credit depends on whether both types of unemployment tax apply to the same wages and the state is not a credit reduction state (one that borrowed money from the federal government to pay unemployment benefits and hasn't repaid it).

Paying FUTA works differently. Any quarter that the FUTA liability reaches $500, the tax payment must be deposited; if your FUTA liability is less than $500, it gets carried over to the next quarter (and possibly the next) until it reaches $500. Most employers are required to use the Electronic Federal Tax Payment System (EFTPS) to make their FUTA tax deposits. If the fourth quarter liability is less than $500, that payment can be paid along with Form 940.

SELF-EMPLOYMENT TAXES

If you earn any money as a 1099 worker or own a small business, you'll be on the hook for self-employment taxes (assuming your net income is at least $400). These are basically Social Security and Medicare (FICA) taxes that would normally be handled by an employer. Since you are your own employer in these circumstances, you're responsible for paying these taxes directly, both the employee and employer portions for a total of 15.3% (12.4% Social Security plus 2.9% Medicare) of your *net* earned income. The self-employment tax is applied to 92.35% of that net income so you don't end up paying tax on the tax (7.65% is half of the total tax).

Since self-employment taxes are not withheld from anything, you have to make proactive quarterly estimated tax payments to take care of them. If your business (and if you're a 1099 worker, you technically have a business) earns any profits, you will owe self-employment taxes even if you don't end up owing any income taxes.

Here's an example with numbers. Suppose your business has a $100,000 profit (for easier math). First, multiply your net profit by 92.35% to determine the taxable amount: $100,000 × 0.9235 = $92,350. Then multiply the result by 15.3% to determine the self-employment tax: $92,350 × 0.153 = $14,130. This will add $3,532 to each quarterly estimated tax payment you make during the year ($14,130 ÷ 4 = $3,532).

Other Payroll Taxes

Depending on where you work, you may have to deal with additional payroll taxes, usually dealing with unemployment or disability funds. These are state-based taxes, so they don't apply to everyone. For example, California requires employees pay state disability insurance taxes, and Alaska, New Jersey, and Pennsylvania all require withholding for state unemployment taxes.

The total self-employment tax gets calculated and reported on IRS Schedule SE as part of your annual personal income tax return. Self-employed individuals can take an above-the-line deduction for half of the self-employment taxes paid for that tax year.

CAPITAL GAINS TAX

You Win, You Pay

When you sell an asset that you own for more money than you paid for it, the IRS calls that a capital gain. An asset is anything you own for personal or investment reasons. That includes everything from your jewelry to your house to stocks and bonds. It doesn't matter how you got the asset, whether you bought it, inherited it, or got it as a gift. When you sell the asset, that sale will result in a capital gain or a capital loss for tax purposes. If you sell it for more than it cost you, you end up with a capital gain. If you sell it for less than it cost you, you end up with a capital loss.

WHAT ARE CAPITAL ASSETS?

Technically, capital assets include anything you own. For tax purposes, capital assets include real and personal (meaning not real estate) property with significant value. Any time you sell a capital asset, the IRS wants to know, so it's important to know what you have. That's especially true for people who sell their used household items on platforms like eBay, even if you don't get back as much as you originally paid for them.

On the personal side, the most common capital assets include real estate, vehicles, household furnishings, artwork, and investments. If you own a business, everything that business owns with a useful life of more than one year also counts as a capital asset. This could include anything from a laptop to a desk to a factory to a rental property, but it wouldn't include things you use up quickly like paper and pens. On the business side, capital assets get depreciated for accounting and tax purposes. That means their value on the books declines steadily over time while you're still using them.

Capital assets can be tangible, meaning they have a physical form, or intangible, meaning things that don't have a physical form but still have lasting value. Intangible assets include stocks, bonds, patents, and copyrights.

IT STARTS WITH BASIS

All capital gains calculations start with basis, the at-cost value of whatever asset you've sold. In its simplest form, basis equals how much you paid for the asset when you bought it. But, like all things tax-related, basis isn't always quite that simple and may involve more math.

A more complete definition would be that basis equals the total cost of acquiring an asset and getting it ready for use. So for an asset like corporate stock, it would be the share price plus any commissions paid plus any other costs involved in acquiring those shares. For an asset like a building, it would include everything paid to buy the property and making it habitable such as closing costs, title costs, or capital improvements (like a new roof or an updated electrical system). You'd also have to subtract things like related tax credits, insurance payouts, or incentives received related to that property.

With investments like stocks, bonds, and funds (mutual funds or exchange-traded funds), it's common to buy shares in batches, and that can also affect the cost basis when you sell shares. For example, if you bought fifty shares of XYZ Corp for $10 each (total $500) in April and fifty shares for $11 each (total $550) in June, your total basis in your one hundred shares of XYZ Corp would be $1,050. If you sold sixty shares in December, you'd have to decide which shares you sold to determine the cost basis for that transaction. That calculated cost basis could range from $610 to $650 depending on which specific shares you sold, which will impact the tax effects of the sale.

Basis rules work differently for assets you didn't buy, like gifts or inheritance. Generally speaking, the basis will be the value of the property when you receive it, but it can get much more complicated than that. If you're gifted or inherit an asset that you plan to sell, it makes sense to talk to a tax advisor to help you figure out the best ways to minimize the potential tax burden.

HOW CAPITAL LOSSES FIT IN

Capital losses occur when you sell an asset for less than its basis—you lost money on the deal. These losses can be taken against any capital gains, reducing those taxes. If you end up losing more than your capital gains, called a net loss, you can use up to $3,000 of those losses to offset your other taxable income. Your net capital loss will work sort of like a tax deduction.

Some financial advisors may recommend a strategy called "tax loss harvesting" when you have higher income or a lot of capital gains. This involves selling assets, usually investments like stocks, that have decreased in value and are not expected to recover. While it never makes sense to sell assets based on the tax effects alone, strategically timing the sale of an asset you were going to get rid of anyway can deliver tax benefits.

THE CAPITAL GAINS TAX

For tax purposes, capital gains are divided into short-term and long-term categories. Short-term capital gains apply to assets held for one year or less, while long-term capital gains apply to assets held for more than one year. That matters because the long-term gains are taxed at lower rates than short-term gains, sometimes as low as no tax at all depending on your overall income level. Short-term gains are taxed at ordinary income tax rates, which typically exceed capital gains rates.

Long-term capital gains are taxed at either 0%, 15%, or 20% depending on your income and tax filing status. These rates and income levels are subject to change, so visit the IRS website at www.irs.gov for the latest information. For 2024, long-term capital gains rates work like this:

CAPITAL GAINS TAX RATE	SINGLE	HEAD OF HOUSEHOLD	MARRIED FILING JOINTLY	MARRIED FILING SEPARATELY
0%	$0 – $47,025	$0 – $63,000	$0 – $94,050	$0 – $47,025
15%	$47,026 – $518,900	$63,001 – $551,350	$94,051 –$583,750	$47,026 – $291,850
20%	More than $518,900	More than $551,350	More than $583,750	More than $291,850

When You Sell Collectibles

Unlike other capital assets, those classified by the IRS as collectibles may face long-term capital gains tax rates of up to 28%. Collectibles here include things like coins, stamps, comics, fine art, and antiques. Short-term gains on collectibles work the same as all short-term capital gains, taxed at ordinary income rates.

PROPERTY TAXES

Bring Me a Shrubbery

Property taxes rank among the oldest taxes levied in all of history, probably because they're the easiest to assess and administer. These days, we don't pay a portion of our harvest or herds, instead ponying up cash every year in relation to the value of any property we own. Property taxes are levied by the states, so there's a lot of variety in the rules and rates. Every state has some form of property tax, even if it's at the county level rather than statewide.

Property taxes can affect both real estate (also called real property) and other types of possessions (called personal property) like cars, boats, and computers. The biggest property tax for most Americans is the one levied on their homes, where the average annual bill comes to $2,869. Vehicle taxes come in second with an average $448 per year for people living in states that charge it.

REAL PROPERTY TAXES

People tend to lump all property tax into a single bucket, but there are actually several kinds of real property–based taxes. Every state has some form of property tax, at least at the local level. The most common form is real estate tax (which most people just call "property tax"), but even that can be split into different types. Some states also have personal property taxes, and we'll cover those later in this section. These taxes are used to fund local and state projects and community services. They support schools, public works, parks, libraries, police, and community pools.

Real estate taxes are levied on real property—land, buildings, land or building improvements, farms, and commercial properties. Many American homeowners are most familiar with the annual taxes assessed on the fair market value of their homes, generally calculated by multiplying that assessment by the state or local tax rate, often called the millage rate.

Renters Pay Too

If you think renters don't pay real estate taxes, think again. While they may not pay those directly, they do pay them indirectly as part of their monthly rent. Because of this, some states (including Colorado, Maryland, and Vermont) offer a renter's tax credit similar to property tax credits.

Some localities split up their real estate taxes into things like school taxes, sanitation or department of public works (DPW) taxes, and special projects. However they label these, if they're based on the value of your real estate, they count as real property taxes. Real estate tax rates range from 0.27% (in Hawaii) to 2.33% (in New Jersey).

PERSONAL PROPERTY TAXES

Some states and localities charge personal property taxes, where personal property includes assets that are not real estate. These taxes are generally used to fund public projects like building schools and parks.

While personal property covers almost everything you have, the tax usually applies only to assets over a certain value. Think cars, jewelry, and computers rather than dishes, throw pillows, and books.

How these assets get taxed depends on the rules of the state or locality imposing them. They choose:

- What gets taxed
- How the personal property gets valued (for example, purchase price or assessed value)
- Whether individuals, businesses, or both will be subject to the tax
- The personal property tax rate
- When and how the taxes must be paid (for example, upon purchase or annually)
- What the funds will be used for

The most commonly charged personal property tax is on vehicles. Twenty-six states have a vehicle tax, ranging from 0.10% (in Louisiana) to 3.97% (in Virginia), according to WalletHub. These are not the same as sales taxes, one-time levies at the time of purchase, as they are charged annually and usually based on the current book value.

Of the states that do have personal property taxes, which include Maryland, California, North Carolina, and others, most assess and bill annually, often on January 1. Some states allow for self-reporting and paying, and this generally also takes place annually. For federal income tax purposes, personal property taxes paid may be included in itemized deductions up to a total of $10,000 for all combined state and local taxes.

PROPERTY TAX ASSESSMENTS

Periodically, usually every year, the state or local government will assess your property, meaning assign a value to it. These are typically based on the appraised value (usually lower than the fair market value), which may look nothing like what you actually paid for the property or what you could get if you sold it today. They come up with that number based on a cost and sales comparison analysis. The cost component involves taking the cost of the land and the expected cost to rebuild the structures on it (such as houses, sheds, garages, or other buildings) less any depreciation. The sales component relies on recent sales of comparable properties.

When you get your assessment in the mail (though you can usually go online to find out your assessment too), it will usually include a detailed description of how they came up with the value and how you can dispute it if you disagree.

PAYING PROPERTY TAXES

Generally, there are two main ways you can pay your real property taxes. The first is paying them directly when you receive your property tax bill, usually annually or semiannually. The second is adding them to your mortgage payments, which lets you spread them over the whole year. The mortgage processor holds those payments in escrow and remits each payment when they are due.

For personal property taxes, these are typically paid when an annual return or report is filed. In some cases, the state will send an annual bill similar to one created for real property.

If you don't pay your property taxes, the state can issue a lien against your property. Tax liens are legal claims on your property. While in most cases the state will not seize your property, they may be legally entitled to a portion of the sale proceeds to settle the claim when you sell the property.

SALES AND USE TAXES

You Buy It, We Tax It

If you've ever bought anything, you've almost certainly paid sales tax. These taxes are paid by the customer purchasing the product or service, collected by the seller, and remitted to the appropriate state or local government entity. These taxes are calculated as a percentage of the purchase price, and rates can vary widely.

Generally, sales taxes are paid by the final purchaser of a product, the end user. Companies that make or procure products for other companies to sell and the retailers who sell them typically have resale certificates and therefore aren't required to pay sales taxes. Some nonprofit organizations or government offices (like schools) may be exempt from paying sales taxes as well. The specific rules depend on the particular state or locality.

STATE BY STATE

There is no federal sales tax in the United States (at least for now). Rather, each state decides whether or not it will have a sales tax, what products and services will be subject to it, and what the rates are. Five states don't charge sales tax at all: Delaware, Alaska, New Hampshire, Oregon, and Montana (although Alaska does allow its localities to charge sales tax). All other states do, and those range from a low of 2.9% in Colorado to a high of 7.25% in California. Those rates don't include any local sales taxes, which pile on to what the state charges.

States also vary in which items they tax, and some of them have superspecific rules about what's subject to sales taxes. For example, in

New York, bagels are subject to sales tax if they're sliced, toasted, or made into sandwiches. Without this preparatory work, there's no sales tax. In Arizona, bags of ice cubes are not subject to sales tax but blocks of ice are. Finally, in California, fruit bought from vending machines is subject to a 33% sales tax, but not fruit bought from grocery stores.

For the most part, necessities like food aren't subject to sales tax. All other products are fair game in the states that impose sales taxes. And for the states that tax services, the lists of what counts as a taxable service vary widely.

FROM A SMALL BUSINESS POINT OF VIEW

Businesses sell products or services and often need to create and remit sales taxes to the states they do business in. This can get extremely confusing and hard to manage for small businesses that operate in multiple states with wildly different sales tax laws and potential penalties for not remitting them properly. You may require professional help or a dedicated sales tax software to manage these taxes correctly.

The first step is to learn the sales tax laws and responsibilities in your state and locality and any other states you sell products in (yes, this includes online sales). You'll need to determine if the particular products you sell or services you offer are taxable. Whether or not your business will be responsible for dealing with sales tax collection depends on if it has a "tax nexus" (meaning a big enough presence) in that state. If it does, the business will have to register with the state's taxing authority, and you'll need to apply for your sales tax permit.

Next, you'll have to figure out the correct tax rate to charge in each state or locality your business has nexus and set up a system to collect it from your customers. Schedules may vary, but most states require monthly or quarterly sales tax reporting and remittance, depending on your sales volume. Again, this can be very tricky to get right, so hire a professional if needed.

THE PERSONAL PERSPECTIVE

Sales taxes make the things you buy cost more, as they're generally added on to the total costs of a purchase at the point of sale. These are regressive taxes, meaning that they have a higher cost for lower-income individuals because they take up a bigger percentage of their income (even though it's the same dollar amount for everyone).

Though "necessities" typically are not subject to sales tax, the definition of what qualifies as a necessity can vary by state. Generally food, medicine, healthcare services, and clothing are exempt from sales taxes, but that's not necessarily true in all states. Plus, many states have taxable categories inside these normally exempt necessities, such as charging sales tax on prepared foods but not whole foods.

UNDERSTANDING USE TAXES

Think of use taxes as the cousin of sales taxes—a back door into making sure residents don't skip out on sales tax. They come into play when you've bought things out of state and didn't pay sales tax but would have if you'd made the purchase in your home state. The use tax rate is typically the same as your state sales tax rate.

Here's an example: Say you live in Maryland, where there's a sales tax on clothes. You shop in Delaware because there's no sales tax and bring the clothes home with you. Since you'll be using the clothes in Maryland and you haven't already paid sales tax on the clothing, you're responsible to report and pay the use tax.

The Pink Tax

Though it's not always in the form of an actual tax, the "pink tax" refers to higher prices for women's products compared to essentially identical men's products. The discriminatory pricing hits items like razors and other personal care goods, clothing, haircuts, and even children's toys. Over a lifetime, the pink tax can add up to serious money—more than $80,000.

Use taxes effectively go by the honor system. People are supposed to calculate and pay use taxes (in the states where they apply). But many (probably most) people don't realize this responsibility even exists, let alone how to go about figuring, filing, and paying use taxes. But states that charge use tax (which is almost every state) have special forms that cover this and expect people to complete them and pay the tax. Like with other types of taxes, failing to report and pay any use taxes can result in interest and penalties for the taxpayer.

GIFT AND ESTATE TAXES

Even Dead People Pay Taxes

There's a lot of confusion surrounding gift and estate taxes (sometimes called death taxes), but the way the rules stand as of 2024, most people won't have to worry about paying them. However, that doesn't mean you'll never be responsible for filing gift or estate tax returns, so it's important to understand how they work. The main misconception with these taxes is who pays the tax, the giver or the receiver. Answer: It's always the person making the gift or the estate itself. That doesn't mean a gift recipient won't have to deal with any tax issues concerning what they received, but it won't be in the form of gift and estate taxes. Gift tax returns get filed by the person making the gift, and estate tax returns are the responsibility of the estate executor.

WHAT ARE GIFT AND ESTATE TAXES?

Gift and estate taxes are transfer taxes that kick in when one person transfers their property to another person for nothing in return. While you're living, transfers are gifts; after you die, your estate makes the transfers. For tax purposes, both types of transfers add together to determine whether your estate will owe any taxes. There's effectively no separate gift tax, but lifetime gifts may get included in the value of the estate.

Under federal law, estate taxes only get levied on estates with assets of more than $13.61 million (the estate tax exemption) based on their fair market value at the time of death. Unless Congress changes it, the estate tax exemption will revert after 2025 to approximately $7 million (the $5.6 million 2017 exemption, increased for inflation), which could lead to many more families owing estate taxes. The tax rates range from 18% to 40% as of 2024. State laws vary widely, with some levying no estate taxes at all, while others charge as much as 20%.

There's a special provision in the IRC that lets anyone transfer any amount of assets to their spouse at any time, in life or death, completely free of transfer taxes. This provision, the unlimited marital deduction, went into effect in 1982. It serves to help surviving spouses preserve family wealth during their lifetime by treating the couple as a single economic unit for estate tax purposes. For example, if you leave everything in your estate (or everything of value that you own like money, property, and furniture) to your spouse, there would be no estate taxes at that time regardless of its value. It effectively delays any potential estate tax until the death of the surviving spouse.

THE GIFT EXCLUSION

Every year, anyone can make gifts up to a specific dollar amount per recipient, known as the annual gift exclusion (sometimes called the gift tax exclusion). That means the excluded gift won't be added back into the estate and won't be subject to transfer taxes. For 2024, the gift limit is $18,000 ($36,000 for married couples). If gifts during the year to any one recipient total more than the limit, you have to file a gift tax return on IRS Form 709. The excess gift will go toward your lifetime gift exclusion of $13.61 million (for 2024), and if you exceed that, then gift taxes will come into play.

Here's how this works in practice. Say you have ten people you want to give gifts to. You can give them each up to $18,000, gifting a total of $180,000, without exceeding your limit or needing to file a gift tax return. However, if you gave one person $20,000, whether it was all at once or in pieces (like two $10,000 gifts), you would have exceeded the $18,000 limit and would need to file a gift tax return. The excess $2,000 would go toward the lifetime exclusion.

However, exceptions include gifts between spouses (which are unlimited), gifts to qualified nonprofit organizations (these count as charitable contributions rather than gifts), and paying for someone's tuition or medical expenses directly (to the institution). Additionally, some things you wouldn't think count as gifts might. For example, if you add someone (other than your spouse) as a joint owner of a bank account where they could withdraw money at any time, that's technically a gift.

Generation Skipping Transfer Tax

Decades ago, wealthy families realized they could skip a generation of taxation by willing estates to their grandchildren instead of their kids. Congress then introduced the Generation Skipping Transfer Tax (GSTT) in 1976, which made it so that the grandchildren inherit only what they would have if the estate had passed to their parents first. So, any time a person makes a transfer, in life or death, to a person who's at least 37.5 years younger than them (but not their spouse), it's considered to be skipping a generation. Plus, the GSTT is a flat 40% tax on the entire taxable estate (the amount that exceeds the lifetime exemption) that's levied in addition to the regular gift and estate tax.

AT THE STATE LEVEL

Estate-based tax rules at the state level vary widely and are imposed in addition to federal gift and estate taxes. They do have a couple of things in common, though: None imposes taxes on estates valued at less than $1 million, and the prevailing state tax law is based on the decedent's home state when they died. States that currently levy an estate tax include Connecticut, Hawaii, Illinois, Maine, Maryland, Massachusetts, Minnesota, New York, Oregon, Rhode Island, Vermont, Washington, and the territory of Washington, DC.

Because many states have lower thresholds than the federal government, an estate exempt from federal estate taxes could still owe state estate taxes. In most cases, if the value of the gross estate (the value of all the property before any expenses are deducted) exceeds the state exemption, an estate tax return will need to be filed even if it doesn't result in taxes due. The estate executor must file the estate tax return.

Six states (Iowa, Kentucky, Nebraska, New Jersey, Maryland, and Pennsylvania) levy inheritance rather than estate taxes, and one state—Maryland—levies both. This tax is typically based on the home state of the person that died, rather than where the heir lives. Specifics, like exemptions and whether direct family is subject to this tax, also vary from state to state. The estate executor is responsible for filing the inheritance tax return and remitting any taxes due from the estate.

Chapter 4

Estimated Tax Payments

Estimated tax payments frustrate and cause anxiety for millions of Americans, including many small business owners, every year. These estimates are a system that was originally designed to capture taxes on predictable income, like rents and pensions, that don't normally have taxes withheld. The basic idea is to know how much tax you're going to owe for the whole year and split that up into four quarterly lump sum payments that you remit to the IRS and the state (if it has income taxes).

This model can work well when income is predictable and relatively steady from one year to the next. But that's not how it works for millions of freelancers, side-giggers, and entrepreneurs in many cases. Income can be unpredictable month to month, let alone year to year. Still, the IRS and the state government expect those quarterly estimated tax payments from anyone who earns any kind of income that doesn't have taxes withheld from it. So taxpayers in this situation need to get familiar with the when and how of estimated tax payments.

WHAT ARE ESTIMATED TAX PAYMENTS?

Are They Just Making This Stuff Up?

When you don't have any taxes withheld from your income, like you would with a paycheck, the IRS expects you to self-pay throughout the year. The self-calculated payments, better known as estimated taxes, get made quarterly, but it's not quite as simple as is sounds.

The current estimated tax payment system the US has is out-dated, created during a time when untaxed income was boringly pre-dictable. Now, with around 16.5 million people having side hustles and small business income that fluctuates throughout the year, it's much harder to calculate estimated tax payments accurately. Unfor-tunately, the IRS doesn't care about that. They're tied to the old ways (by law), and expect people to make accurate, timely, and *equal* pay-ments on every due date. (However, there is a way around this, as you'll see later in this chapter.) That's why it's so important to know if you have to make estimated tax payments and how to figure out how much to pay, and remember to make them every quarter on time.

WITHOUT WITHHOLDING

If you earn any income at all that does not have withholding taxes taken out of it, you may need to make estimated tax payments. Many people don't realize this, thinking that the taxes coming out of their paychecks will cover their total bill. Unfortunately, they're surprised when they do their taxes and realize they owe a lot of money.

There are a wide variety of common income sources that are not typically subject to withholding taxes, such as 1099 income for non-employee compensation, small business profits, rental income, royalties, affiliate income, investment income like dividends and interest, capital gains, and retirement account withdrawals.

In some cases, you may be able to have taxes withheld so you can avoid the hassle of remembering to make estimated tax payments. But for most of these types of income, it will be up to you to figure out how much more you'll owe and make the appropriate payments.

WHAT YOU THINK YOU'LL OWE

Taxpayers are expected to make estimated tax payments when they'll end up owing at least $1,000 at tax time. If your income is relatively steady, figuring out estimated taxes can be straightforward. Things like rental income, dividends, and pension payments are generally predictable. That gives you a reasonable idea of how much additional taxable income you'll have, so it's just a matter of applying the appropriate tax rates.

Unpredictable income can be harder to manage, especially for new business owners or affiliate marketers who don't yet have a sense of what their actual annual revenues and expenses will be. Do your best to work out a reasonable estimate of the sales and expenses so you can figure out potential profits, adjusting throughout the year as the real numbers take shape. Plus, if you have any self-employment income, you'll need to factor self-employment taxes into your calculation. Even if you don't think you'll end up owing income taxes, you may still owe self-employment taxes.

Other items may be unpredictable at the beginning of the year, but you'll know their impact when they occur. For example, if you sell an investment and make a profit, you'll know exactly how much you gained once the transaction takes place. Or if you take an unexpected withdrawal from a retirement account, you'll know how much that adds to your income and whether you'll be subject to the additional 10% penalty.

Remember: It's okay to adjust your estimated payments mid-year. You may still be subject to some penalties, but the closer you get to the actual tax total, the less you'll have to pay when you file your tax return.

Even If Your Job Withholds Taxes

Most people with regular W-2 jobs will pay enough in withholding taxes during the year. However, some people fill out their W-4s incorrectly, some get bonuses or special compensation that throws the taxes off, and some have other income that's enough to cause a balance due. Do a mid-year tax check-in to make sure your withholding is enough to cover your tax bill before it's too late to do something about it.

STATES REQUIRE THIS TOO

If you need to make federal estimated tax payments, chances are you'll need to make estimated payments to the state (or states) as well. Most states with income tax require these quarterly payments if you'll end up owing more than their stated amount. For example, if you'll end up owing more than $300 in New York or $400 in Massachusetts, you have to make estimated tax payments. The most common cutoff amount is $1,000 followed by the next most popular of $500. You'll need to check with your state taxing authority to find out the applicable amount there. If you'll owe taxes in multiple states, make sure to find out the requirements for each.

AIM FOR ZERO

Coming up with accurate estimates is important for two reasons:

1. You don't want to owe a lot of money plus interest and penalties when you file your tax return.
2. You don't want to give the IRS a huge interest-free loan for the year and get a big refund when you could have been using that money yourself all year long.

Good estimates aim for zero, no balance due and no refund. Of course, that rarely (if ever) happens, so you want to aim for as close to zero as possible. That takes a little work, but it's worth it. A reasonably realistic estimate helps you avoid paying the IRS more than you really owe due to added penalties and interest. At the same time, it stops you from overpaying and having less money available to you throughout the year.

WHY DO YOU HAVE TO PAY ESTIMATED TAXES?

To Get to the Other Side

The United States income tax system is "pay as you go." That means you have to pay taxes on your income throughout the whole year as you earn it. Technically, you're supposed to pay level amounts into your tax account to go toward your final balance even though you may not know at the beginning of the year how much you'll owe by the end of the year. For most Americans, employers take care of this tax prepayment by withholding income and payroll taxes from their paychecks, and then remitting them to the federal and applicable state governments throughout the year.

When you have income that doesn't have taxes withheld (like they are with most jobs) or don't have enough taxes withheld, you have to proactively make tax payments yourself instead. Rather than submitting payments every time you get income, you're only required to submit estimated tax payments four times a year. These payments go toward your final tax bill, the same way as the total tax withheld on a W-2 would be.

THE POINT OF ESTIMATED TAX PAYMENTS

Like your household, the US government runs on a budget. They base their budget on the amount of tax revenue they expect to receive both for the year and throughout the year. They try to match up the money coming in with the money going out. Withholding taxes from paychecks is steady and predictable, making it easy to plan. Estimated tax payments only come in four times during the year, giving an extra cash infusion each quarter.

The government relies on those estimated tax bumps in its quarterly budgets, knowing that the biggest bump will come on April 15. Both prior year tax balances and current year first quarter estimated tax payments are due on this date.

There's an IRS Tool for This

The IRS offers an "Am I required to make estimated tax payments?" tool on their website. They claim it takes about ten minutes to complete all the questions, but it takes many taxpayers longer. The question list can be extensive based on your answers, and they expect you to know a lot about income you haven't received yet. Many people find it easier to ask their tax pro or check their tax software than to try to deal with this IRS tool.

The IRS bases their expectations for estimated tax payments on prior year tax returns, expecting the revenue to be similar. However, people's income varies much more now than it did historically, leading to much more unpredictable income for both citizens and tax collectors. Even if your income is hard to predict, you still need to make good faith estimated tax payments if you want to avoid issues with the IRS.

CONSEQUENCES OF NOT PAYING

If you don't make estimated tax payments, you'll get hit with a few financial consequences, some involving paying even *more* money to the IRS. Others involve potential financial hardship for you and your family. If you can make even partial estimated tax payments, you likely should.

When you don't make estimated tax payments during the year, you'll end up owing much more tax money when you file your income tax return. Essentially, that means you'll have to come up with a much bigger lump sum in April. If you don't have the full balance handy, you might end up borrowing money to pay it, which will result in interest charges. If you simply don't pay it, you'll also be subject to IRS interest and penalties. However, you should be aware that even if you do pay in full through estimated tax payments, even if you actually overpay, you could still be subject to IRS interest and penalties for not paying all four quarterly estimates during the year.

Many people struggle to come up with the quarterly estimate payments, especially when they're self-employed and dealing with the self-employment taxes along with the income taxes. Even if you can't pay the full estimate you think you'll owe, anything you pay in is better than nothing. Also, make sure to make that estimated tax payment by the due date. It will reduce the eventual amount you owe as well as reducing interest charged on the underpayment.

PUT MONEY ASIDE

Since estimated tax payments are supposed to mirror withholding taxes, one strategy that may help is to put aside money every time you receive income. Some people set up separate bank accounts (preferably high-yield savings accounts) for this purpose and transfer a set percentage in whenever they get paid. Take into consideration the type of income, your marginal federal tax rate, and potential state taxes when figuring out how much to save. For example, if you earn money as a landlord, you could stash 20%–25% of every rent payment received in your tax account every month. If you work as a freelancer, you could transfer 30%–35% of every client payment into your tax account when you receive it; the savings rate is higher because of the additional self-employment taxes.

Marginal Tax Rates

Marginal tax rates are the percent of taxes paid on the next dollar of income you earn, based on your tax bracket. As your income increases and moves into higher tax brackets, each additional dollar of your earnings will be taxed at the next highest rate. For example, if you're a single taxpayer and your total income just passed $47,150, the *next* $53,375 of income you earn would be taxed at 22%.

It sounds like a lot to divert toward taxes, and it is. Taxes take up a huge chunk of your income. You don't notice it as much with regular paychecks because the taxes are already out when you receive them. Making a habit of self-withholding will help make sure you have enough cash available when tax payments come due.

WHO HAS TO PAY ESTIMATES?

Don't Skip This Step

Anyone who receives income without taxes taken out will probably need to make estimated tax payments. That may include sources like investment income, interest, withdrawals from retirement accounts, business income, and rental income.

In some cases, people who do have taxes withheld might need to make estimated tax payments, if they aren't withholding enough and need to make up the difference. This could happen if their income includes things like stock options and bonuses, for example. You might also need to pay more if your life circumstances change during the year, like getting divorced, but you haven't made changes to your W-4 to reflect that.

If you're not sure whether you might have to make an estimated tax payment, do a tax checkup during the year. You can do that by adding up all of your expected income, subtracting your expected deductions, and applying the current year's tax rates to get a general sense of how much your total tax bill might be. Compare that to what you've paid in, and if you haven't paid enough you can make an estimated tax payment.

SMALL BUSINESS OWNERS

If you're a small business owner and your company is set up as anything other than a C corporation, you'll have to make personal quarterly estimated tax payments on the business income. (The C corporation is responsible for making its own quarterly estimated tax payments, which you'll probably have to manage separately.) That's because all other types of business income pass through to your personal tax return.

More types of workers than you'd think fit into this small business category, which includes people with side gigs, freelancers, consultants, and independent contractors (that is, the incorrectly named "1099 employees"). Any work that you get paid for *other than as an employee* counts as business income.

You can deduct all of your legitimate business expenses against any income you earn this way. If you don't take full advantage of your expense deductions, you'll pay more in taxes than you actually owe—and no one wants to do that. Make sure to carefully track all of your expenses and keep detailed records of them (in case you were to get audited). There's no reason to not deduct every possible allowable expense to reduce your tax bill every year.

In addition to regular income tax, you will owe an additional 15.3% in self-employment taxes on your net income. That's the combined employee and employer portions of Social Security and Medicare taxes. Your estimated tax payments will include the combination of income and self-employment taxes.

LANDLORDS

If you own any rental property, including short-term rentals like Airbnb or Vrbo, and it's making money, you'll need to make estimated tax payments. Like with businesses, you can deduct expenses related to the rental income, which can lower your overall tax burden. Unlike businesses, rental income is considered passive and generally not subject to self-employment taxes, but these taxes may come into play. If, as a landlord, you provide "substantial services" (such as cleaning while the property is occupied, changing linens for guests, and acting as a concierge) to your renters, which often happens with short-term rentals, that income may cross the line into active earnings.

Any profitable property will generate an income tax bill, possibly with self-employment taxes tacked on. Since none of those earnings from the property have had taxes withheld, you'll be responsible for making quarterly estimated tax payments based on your net rental income.

INVESTORS

Income you earn from your non-retirement investments typically doesn't have any taxes withheld and could generate the need for estimated tax payments. Investments can generate both income taxes and capital gains taxes, which come with different tax rates. You need to pay tax on the earnings generated by your investments, even if you don't actually get any money.

Interest income, which is money earned from bank deposits, is generally taxed at regular income tax rates. However, some types of interest income, like interest on municipal bonds, are exempt from federal income taxes.

Dividends, which are distributions made to corporate shareholders, are taxed based on their type: ordinary or qualified. Ordinary dividends get taxed at your regular income tax rates. Qualified dividends get taxed at capital gains rates, which are generally lower.

Capital gains occur when you sell investments for more than you originally paid to buy them. The tax rates for capital gains depend on three factors: how long you held the investment before selling, your income, and your filing status. Short-term capital gains occur when you sell an investment you've held for one year or less, and those are taxed at ordinary income rates. Long-term capital gains (investments held longer than one year) get taxed at beneficial capital gains rates based on your income and filing status. Long-term capital gains rates (for 2024) range from 0% to 20%. Some investments like mutual funds may also generate capital gains.

If you have significant investment income, you probably need to make estimated tax payments. Knowing which type of tax goes with which type of income can help you figure out how much you'll owe, allowing you to make reasonable payments throughout the year.

RETIREMENT ACCOUNT WITHDRAWALS

When you pull money out of traditional retirement accounts like IRAs and 401(k)s, you (generally) have to pay tax on the full withdrawal. If you take the money out before age fifty-nine and a half, you may also have to pay a 10% early withdrawal penalty on top of the regular income taxes. That additional taxable income not only adds to your tax bill; it may also push you into a higher tax bracket.

Some workplace-based plans like 401(k)s automatically withhold 20% for federal income taxes. With IRAs, you may have to request withholding. If you didn't have any money withheld from your withdrawals, you'll need to make estimated tax payments to cover the higher tax bill. And even if you did request withholding, it may not be enough to cover the full taxes due on the withdrawal.

FIGURING OUT WHAT TO PAY

More Math?

It's easy when money for taxes is automatically taken out of your paycheck every pay period, but it's more complicated when you have to figure it out yourself and make payments every quarter. You have to consider all your income, deductions, and applicable tax credits to figure out your eventual tax bill. It's almost like doing your taxes ahead of time. Plus, if your untaxed income is unpredictable, it can be extra tricky to calculate the right amount to pay.

To get close to the right number, you'll have to do some math. The IRS has a worksheet you can use as part of its Form 1040-ES (the form you use to make estimated tax payments) instructions. It requires a lot of information and some math to come up with a realistic estimate, so gather up your info before you get started. If your income situation is pretty similar to last year, you can use your prior total tax (not the amount you owed) as a good starting point. If your income sources and amounts have changed significantly, or if you've had a major life change (like marriage, adoption, or home ownership), you'll need to involve a little more guesswork as you perform the calculations.

ESTIMATED TAX MATH

When your income is predictable and you know it will be similar to last year's, you can use last year's total tax as a model for this year's estimated tax payments. It's that simple: Pay 100% of last year's total tax (not just the amount you owed in April), and you at least won't have to face underpayment penalties.

When your income varies a lot or your situation has changed, you'll need to do more math to come up with a solid estimate. The first thing you have to figure out is how much gross income you expect to earn for the whole year. That means adding up all your sources of income; this is anything from your paycheck to side gig earnings to the interest on your high-yield savings account to any money you pulled out of a retirement plan. You want to make sure to include your paycheck even though taxes have already been taken out because you need to know the gross income amount to determine your tax bracket. Remember not to include nontaxable money like child support, loan proceeds, or garage sales (as long as you don't get more for something than you originally paid for it).

Along with your total gross income, you'll want to figure out your total net self-employment income if you have any. In addition to the income taxes, you'll need to figure out your expected self-employment taxes to come up with your total tax bill.

Next, you will add up items that reduce your gross income. These include things like traditional IRA contributions, self-employed retirement plan contributions, a self-employed health insurance deduction, half of self-employment taxes, and a student loan interest deduction. The total of those items will get subtracted from your gross income to come up with your estimated adjusted gross income (AGI). Once you know the expected AGI, subtract either your expected itemized deductions (use last year's tax return as a guideline, if possible) or the applicable standard deduction. That math brings you to your expected taxable income for the year.

Next step: Look up the IRS tax tables on www.irs.gov to find your tax rates. You can also find those rates as part of the instructions for Form 1040-ES (the form you fill out if you send your payment by mail). Make sure to use the correct tax table based on your filing status. Apply the tax rates to your income to come up with your total estimated income tax bill for the year. If you also need to pay self-employment taxes, add them now to come up with your final total tax.

Your next step will be to add up all of the tax credits that apply to you. Those may include the Child Tax Credit, Earned Income Tax Credit, Child and Dependent Care Tax Credit, or education tax credits (such as the American Opportunity Tax Credit). Once you have those totaled up, you'll subtract them from the total tax. You can also subtract the total amount of withholding taxes you expect to pay for the year if you (or your spouse) have a W-2 job. If your bottom-line number here is greater than $1,000, divide it by four and make four estimated tax payments on the due dates.

Form 1040-ES comes with complete instructions, tax tables, and worksheets to help you figure this all out. You can find Form 1040-ES on the IRS website at www.irs.gov.

If you have to pay state estimated taxes, you'll only have to repeat the tax-related steps with the rules applicable to your state (or states). Your total taxable income will usually be the same (unless you live in more than one state during the year). You can multiply that by your state tax rate, divide by four, and make your quarterly state estimated tax payments.

WHEN YOUR SITUATION CHANGES

Changes in income types and amounts can lead to big differences in required estimated tax payments, but they're not the only things that can affect the estimated balance due. Your life situation plays into this calculation as well. Your tax situation will be influenced by changes in your everyday life including getting married or divorced, having or adopting a baby, the death of a family member, children getting older (turning thirteen or seventeen or ceasing to be dependents), buying or selling a house, an extreme medical situation, a job loss, or starting a side gig/business.

Annualized Income Installment Method

The IRS offers an option for taxpayers with uneven or unpredictable income to help minimize (even eliminate) penalties called the annualized income installment method. This system allows the taxpayer to recalculate estimated tax payments so they match up better to income as it is earned. Each period, the actual income gets annualized to refigure the estimated total tax. At tax time, Form 2210 must be filed along with the tax return.

These are not the only life changes that can affect your tax return, but they are among the most common. Not only might these change your taxable income, but they can also affect deductions and tax credits, which would also impact your total taxes.

MAKING PAYMENTS

Hand Over Your Money

When it comes to making estimated tax payments, your best bet is doing it online through the IRS website or with the IRS2Go app. The IRS agency is understaffed, overworked, and far behind on processing paper forms and payments, so there's no telling when a physical check might be opened and applied to your account, even if you mail it in by the due date.

The most important thing to remember here: Make your estimated tax payments on time. Even if you can't make the full payment, it's better to make a partial payment on time than a full payment a few months later. So pay what you can, when you can. Every dollar you pay in estimated taxes means you'll owe less at tax time and you'll be hit with smaller penalties and interest charges.

HOW TO PAY ONLINE

When you're paying online, you have two options: Use your personal IRS account (https://irs.gov/account) or go through the IRS payment page (https://irs.gov/payments). Either way, you want to make sure to select all the correct choices so your payment gets credited properly:

- Choose "Estimated Tax" under "Reason for Payment."
- Choose "1040 ES" for "Apply Payment to."
- Choose the current tax year (even if it's a different actual year) for "Tax Period for Payment." For example, if you're making the final estimated tax payment for 2024 in 2025, make sure you choose 2024 or your payment will be applied to the wrong tax year.

If you're using the payment page rather than your account page, you'll need some information on hand from the last tax return that you filed. You'll need to know your filing status from that year and your name and address from that year, even if they're different than the current information. They have to match whatever was on your reference return.

One note for married couples who file jointly: Whichever of you is making the online payment, use the account information for the name that appears first on the tax return. Though technically it should work for whichever name and Social Security number you use, many payments have been misapplied when using the "spouse" information (the name that appears second) instead.

You Can Split Your Payments

You don't have to wait until the next quarterly due date to make estimated tax payments. If it's easier for you to make monthly or even weekly payments toward your total estimate instead of paying one huge lump sum, you can do that. Just make sure that you pay the full quarterly amount by the due date.

IF YOU MAIL YOUR PAYMENTS

As previously mentioned, the IRS can take a long time to deal with paper checks. That can cause issues when you file your taxes and claim those payments that the IRS has not officially received, so it's usually in your best interest to avoid this option whenever you can.

If you opt for the mail-in method, you'll need to download and print IRS Form 1040-ES payment vouchers, one for each quarter of the tax year. Make sure the voucher is for the correct tax year and quarter before you complete it. You'll need to fill in all the required information to make sure the IRS is able to apply your payment correctly. That includes the exact amount you're paying, your full name, your Social Security number, and your spouse's name and their Social Security number (if you're married and file a joint return).

Write your check out to "US Treasury" for the exact amount that appears on the payment voucher. Make sure to also write your Social Security number and "XXXX Form 1040-ES," where "XXXX" is the correct tax year (the same as the year on the voucher)—for example, "2025 Form 1040-ES." Do not attach the check to the voucher.

Address the envelope to the appropriate IRS office. You can find a list of office addresses, which are based on where you live, in the instructions for Form 1040-ES. For example, if you live in Montana, you'd send your estimated tax payment to the IRS office in Cincinnati, but if you live in Tennessee, you'd send it to the office in Charlotte.

Before you mail the check, make sure to copy (or take pictures of) the check, the addressed envelope, your payment voucher, and the mailing receipt or postmarked envelope. It's also important to use some form of tracking, like certified mail, when you send it. That way you can prove you mailed the payment on time even if the IRS hasn't gotten around to processing it yet. The IRS counts the payment as made on the postmark date, so make sure to mail the payments by the quarterly due dates.

You'll still probably get an underpayment notice from the agency, and it will still be a hassle to deal with it. But if you can provide evidence of your payment, you'll be able to disagree with the agency and avoid interest and penalties.

BUMP UP WITHHOLDING
WHERE YOU CAN

If the thought of dealing with quarterly estimates feels overwhelming, you may have another option: Increase or request withholding taxes on your income. If you (or your spouse, when you file jointly) have any W-2 income, you can request to have additional withholding taken out of your paycheck. That strategy offers some distinct advantages. First, it spreads the payments out over the whole year instead of requiring you to have the cash to pay four lump sums. Next, even if you only do this for a few months of the year, the IRS still counts it as if you'd made equal payments throughout the whole year. That's in contrast to estimated tax payments, which only count on the day and in the amount they're paid, which can lead to unexpected interest and penalties. You also have more flexibility here, with the ability to change your withholding at any time as your income changes during the year.

If you don't have any W-2 income, you might still be able to request withholding for some of your income. Withdrawals from retirement accounts, for example, are a good source to start with. If you take any money out of your retirement account, you can request that the custodian withhold taxes; usually at least 10%–20% does the trick. Some investment institutions will also withhold taxes on regular investment income, like interest and dividends.

WHAT HAPPENS IF YOU GET IT WRONG?

Everyone Makes Mistakes

For many taxpayers, calculating estimated taxes correctly can be frustrating or difficult, and it can be frightening to think about the consequences of paying the wrong amount of taxes. That's especially true for small business owners with unpredictable earnings throughout the year or taxpayers who haven't managed to save up enough money to meet their estimated tax payment obligations.

Rest assured that while you may face penalties and interest for not paying enough or on time, they won't be as bad as you think. In some cases, the IRS may even waive penalties associated with estimated tax payments. The trick is to have a solid estimate, pay as much as you can of each quarter's estimated payment, and pay it by the due date. That way you can at least reduce the potential penalties and interest that the agency may charge.

IF YOU PAY TOO MUCH

If you pay too much in estimated tax payments, it works the same way as if you'd had too much tax withheld. When you file your tax return, your payments for the year will exceed your balance due and you'll be entitled to a refund. At that point, you can decide whether you'd like to get the money back or to apply it to the next year's estimated tax payments.

In this situation, it makes sense to recalculate the next year's expected estimated tax payments. While getting a refund feels better than owing money, it means that you've given the IRS an interest-free loan. Instead of using that money to further your own financial security, they get to use it. So you will lose out on potential interest or investment income, may end up needing to put more expenses on credit cards, and won't be able to stash away as much money in regular or retirement savings.

You'll want to revisit your estimates and try to get as close to your actual eventual tax bill as possible. If your income and filing situation for the coming tax year is the same as the past year, you may want to reduce your estimated payments to avoid overpaying your taxes. You can always check in with your tax professional if you're unsure how much to pay.

UNDERPAYMENT PENALTIES

When you don't make a sufficient estimated tax payment in any quarter, even if you end up paying enough for the year, you'll be subject to the Underpayment of Estimated Tax by Individuals Penalty. This penalty may also apply if you pay the right amount but your payment is late.

The IRS calculates these penalties based on three factors: the total amount underpaid, the time period of the underpayment, and the IRS interest rate for underpayments (published quarterly). The IRS charges interest on these penalties. That interest gets added to the amount you owe, and it gets charged until you pay the full balance.

You can see if you'll owe a penalty and calculate the amount on IRS Form 2210 while you're preparing your tax return. You can pay the amount you calculated along with your balance due. Or you can have the IRS calculate it for you, which could result in higher penalties and interest (because of the time delay).

Removing or Reducing Penalties

If you do end up owing the IRS a penalty for underpaying estimated taxes, there are things you can do to have the penalty reduced or even removed completely. The IRS has some discretion here. They'll often waive first-time penalties if taxpayers just ask them to.

If you have a good reason for not making a required payment or not paying enough, you can also ask for removal or reduction. To the IRS, reasonable cause includes casualty events, disasters, serious illness or injury to you or a member of your immediate family, or the death of an immediate family member.

Not having enough money to pay doesn't constitute reasonable cause here. Neither do mistakes or relying on professional advice or information, even if that information actually came from the IRS. But if you retired (after age sixty-two) or became disabled during the year and didn't make payments for a reason other than "willful neglect," contact the IRS; they may work with you on at least reducing the penalties.

Taxpayers who had uneven and unpredictable income during the year may be able to use the annualized income installment method. As long as the total payments (even if they're not four equal payments) meet IRS requirements, underpayment penalties may be waived or reduced.

Safe Harbor

To help taxpayers avoid some penalties, the IRS offers a safe harbor strategy. Generally, you can sidestep penalties for underpayment of estimated taxes by paying the lesser of at least 90% of the current year's tax or 100% of the prior year's tax. Since it can be tricky to know what the current year's total will be during the year, it's often safer to pay the same as last year's tax unless you're earning substantially less in the current year. Remember, even under the safe harbor plan the IRS still expects you to make four equal timely estimated tax payments throughout the year.

The penalty rules are different for some high-income taxpayers, and there are also special rules for people who earn at least two-thirds of their income as farmers or fishermen. For taxpayers with AGI more than $150,000 in the prior tax year, the safe harbor amount is the lower of 90% of the current year's tax or 110% of the prior year's total tax. For farmers and fishermen, the safe harbor amount is 66.667% of the current year's tax or 100% of the prior year's tax.

Prioritize Tax Payments When You Can

If you are able to make estimated tax payments and still meet your basic living expenses, it's absolutely best to prioritize those tax payments. But if making an estimated tax payment means you can't make rent, buy groceries, or go to the doctor, it's better to pay the tax penalty. Yes, you will still have to find a way to pay the taxes, but the IRS offers options that landlords and grocery stores don't.

Chapter 5

Money-Saving Tax Strategies

When it comes to paying taxes, you don't want to—and don't have to—pay more than your fair share. But to make sure you don't pay too much, you'll need to know about all of the available deductions, credits, and other tax-savings strategies legally available to you. Remember: Tax *evasion* (intentionally not paying taxes you owe) is a crime, but tax *avoidance*—legally lowering your tax bill—is just a smart financial move.

There are many ways to reduce your tax burden, and each strategy depends on a combination of the type of tax and your unique situation. Some of these are simple enough to DIY, others require—absolutely require—professional help.

You can make significant cuts to your annual tax bills by taking advantage of all the income tax deductions and credits that you qualify for, making tactical use of tax-advantaged accounts, employing special strategies for rental properties and investments, and knowing the ins and outs of minimizing property and sales taxes. Each of these strategies is essential in saving you money in the long haul.

INCOME TAX DEDUCTIONS

Do You Even Know What a Write-Off Is?

Tax deductions reduce your taxable income, and less income means lower taxes. However, the deductions do not mean you'll get a dollar-for-dollar return. A $100 tax deduction would *not* mean your tax bill will be $100 less, just that you'll pay taxes on $100 less.

Everyone who files an individual income tax return gets at least one deduction—the standard deduction—but many people end up with more deductions than that. Different types of deductions have different effects on your overall tax bill, and knowing the differences between these types of deductions can help you prioritize those that will deliver a bigger tax-saving impact.

TAKING ABOVE-THE-LINE DEDUCTIONS

The most valuable tax deductions are above-the-line deductions, meaning they reduce your income before the calculation for AGI. That's why they're called "above-the-line": They appear on your tax return above the line for adjusted gross income. Since many other deductions and credits are limited by AGI, using these special deductions to lower AGI may help you gain eligibility for other lucrative tax-saving measures. Some examples of these are:

- **Student loan interest:** Taxpayers with qualified student loans may be able to deduct the interest paid on those loans, up to

$2,500 per year. This deduction phases out based on your modified adjusted gross income, or MAGI (MAGI is calculated based on this deduction, and this deduction depends on MAGI), and the limits change annually. The IRS has a tool for this called "Can I claim a deduction for student loan interest?" on www.irs.gov.

- **Retirement contributions:** If you contributed to a traditional IRA, you can deduct that with this category. This deduction could be limited if you (or your spouse, if filing jointly) have access to a workplace retirement plan and your income exceeds the IRS limits.

- **Educator expenses:** Educators can deduct up to $300 ($600 if married filing jointly and both are teachers) of money you paid for classroom supplies or similar expenses. This deduction is available for K–12 teachers, counselors, and principals who work at least nine hundred hours during the school year. Qualifying expenses include things like books, software, equipment, and professional development courses.

- **Self-employed health insurance:** If you're self-employed and pay for your own health insurance, you may be able to deduct the full year's premiums with this deduction. You can't take it if you had access to an employer-based plan (including through your spouse). But if you had no other option and paid your own health premiums, you can deduct your medical, dental, and vision insurance and possibly long-term care premiums.

- **Half of self-employment tax:** Self-employed taxpayers get hit with the 15.3% self-employment tax, and half of that can be taken as an above-the-line deduction. If you file Schedule SE (the form that calculates and reports any self-employment taxes due) with your tax return, you'll be able to deduct 50% of the calculated tax here, with no restrictions based on income or outside factors.

You can claim above-the-line deductions along with your standard or itemized deductions.

THE STANDARD DEDUCTION

The standard deduction reduces adjusted gross income by a specific amount so that every household will have at least some income that's not subject to federal income taxes—no questions asked. The amount of the standard deduction depends on your filing status, age, dependency status, and whether or not you're blind. The deduction gets subtracted from your AGI to get to your taxable income.

For tax year 2024, the standard deductions based on filing status are:

FILING STATUS	STANDARD DEDUCTION
Single	$14,600
Head of Household	$21,900
Married Filing Jointly	$29,200
Married Filing Separately	$14,600

Taxpayers who are over the age of sixty-five or blind can take additional standard deductions. Single taxpayers who are over sixty-five or blind get an extra $1,950 standard deduction, and an extra $3,900 if they're over sixty-five and blind. Married taxpayers who are over sixty-five or blind get an extra $1,550 standard deduction each, and an extra $3,100 each if they're over sixty-five and blind.

Dependents—meaning people who are claimed as dependents on someone else's tax return—get a reduced standard deduction. The reduced deduction is either a flat $1,300 or their earned income (such as from a job) plus $450 but not to exceed the regular standard deduction.

In some cases, a taxpayer may not be allowed to take the standard deduction. The most common situation is for those who are married and filing separately, where if one spouse itemizes, they both must itemize. Other circumstances include filing for a short tax year (less than twelve months) because of an accounting change or filing as a nonresident alien.

ITEMIZED DEDUCTIONS

Unlike the standard deduction, which is the same for everyone, itemized deductions vary greatly by each taxpayer's personal situation. These itemized deductions capture expenses paid for during the year that can be used to reduce taxable income and taxes owed. They get listed—itemized—on Schedule A and filed along with your Form 1040. You can choose to take itemized deductions in any tax year that would give you a bigger tax break than using the standard deduction. Plus, you can switch back and forth from year to year.

As of 2024, the big five itemized deductions (most commonly taken) are: unreimbursed medical expenses in excess of 7.5% of AGI; state and local taxes (SALT) up to $10,000; charitable donations up to 60% of AGI; interest for mortgage loans up to $750,000 (used to buy, build, or substantially improve your home); and unreimbursed casualty and theft losses from federally declared disasters that exceed 10% of your AGI.

There are some other allowable itemized deductions that may apply in certain situations. For example, you can deduct gambling losses to the extent of gambling winnings included in your income and impairment-related work expenses for people with disabilities.

There are additional rules for all of the itemized deductions and details on what can and can't be included in each category, and what records are required by the IRS (in case you get audited). You can find full details in the instructions for Schedule A on the IRS website at www.irs.gov.

Little-Known Deductible Medical Expenses

Along with payments for doctors, dentists, and prescriptions, a lot of other medical expenses qualify for this itemized deduction. They include glasses or contacts, service animals, mileage for going to appointments, travel and transportation costs, acupuncture, and chiropractors. Make sure to include everything you can to get the most out of this deduction.

INCOME TAX CREDITS

They're Like Coupons for Taxes

When it comes to taxes, there's nothing you want more than tax credits. These are dollar-for-dollar reductions to your tax bill. A $100 tax credit means you owe $100 less to the IRS.

Tax credits also come with a lot of conditions for taxpayers to meet—they're not available to everyone. Congress creates tax credits to encourage specific behaviors (like buying electronic vehicles) or to support social policies (like lifting families out of poverty). The IRS oversees the tax credits, often looking over tax returns that include them more carefully. That doesn't mean people who qualify shouldn't take the credits. But it does mean that if you take credits when you don't meet all of the eligibility requirements, the IRS will know. So, make sure you take an extra look at the requirements before you take them.

CHILD-RELATED TAX CREDITS

Several popular tax credits revolve around children; these were designed to provide a financial break for families. There are three main direct credits in this category: the Child Tax Credit, the Child and Dependent Care Credit, and the Adoption Credit.

The Child Tax Credit (CTC) is a nonrefundable tax credit for taxpayers with qualifying children younger than seventeen (as of December 31 of the tax year) who have valid Social Security numbers. Some families may qualify for the refundable portion—the Additional Child Tax Credit (ACTC)—based on their income. The maximum CTC is $2,000 per qualifying child, with the ACTC portion of $1,600 each. Both credits begin to phase out for taxpayers with MAGI over $200,000 ($400,000 if married filing jointly). To take advantage of these credits, you must complete Schedule 8812 as part of your tax return.

The Child and Dependent Care Credit is available for working taxpayers who pay for childcare for children under age thirteen (or a disabled dependent of any age). The credit is based on expenses you paid to a qualified caregiver so you were able to work, look for a job, or go to school. The maximum expense for one qualifying child is $3,000, and $6,000 for two or more qualifying children. If you receive dependent care benefits from your employer, you have to deduct that from the childcare expenses you paid. Depending on your AGI, the credit ranges from 20% to 35% of the expenses. To take the credit, you have to identify the caregivers, including their tax ID numbers (spouses and your older dependent children don't qualify). You must complete Form 2441 to take this credit.

Credit for Other Dependents

If you have dependents over age seventeen, like a college-age child or a parent, you may be able to claim the Credit for Other Dependents (ODC). This nonrefundable $500 tax credit covers people you support and can claim as dependents on your tax return other than minor children.

The Adoption Tax Credit is a nonrefundable credit used to offset the costs of adoption. You can receive a tax credit for all of the qualified adoption-related expenses you paid up to $16,810. The credit begins to phase out when your MAGI reaches $252,150. While this credit is not refundable, the unused portion can be carried forward for up to five years. To claim this credit, you'll complete and file Form 8839 with your tax return.

EARNED INCOME TAX CREDIT

The Earned Income Tax Credit (EITC) is a refundable tax credit for low-income taxpayers. Even if you don't owe any taxes and wouldn't otherwise need to file, you can still get this money, assuming you meet all the requirements. Be aware that filing for this credit can delay your tax refund by several weeks, but it can be worth the wait for eligible taxpayers.

Taxpayers may qualify for the EITC if they have earned income, are US citizens/resident aliens, have valid Social Security numbers, are at least twenty-five years old and younger than sixty-five, are not claimed as someone else's dependent or child for the EITC, don't have more than $11,600 in investment income (for 2024), and don't have an income exceeding IRS limits for the family size.

The income limits change every year, and they're based on family size. The highest limits go to married couples (filing jointly) with at least three qualifying children. Qualifying children must live with you for at least half the year, be younger than nineteen (twenty-four if they're in school full-time) and include your children, stepchildren, foster kids, grandchildren, sisters, brothers, nieces, and nephews. You can find all the details of annual income limits and qualifying children on the IRS website at www.irs.gov.

The maximum EITC (for tax year 2024) ranges from $632 for taxpayers with no children to $7,830 to families with at least three children. Though many taxpayers qualify for this tax credit, many don't get it simply because they don't file tax returns. It's worth filing—even if you don't need to—just to get this money back.

SAVER'S CREDIT

The Saver's Credit offers a tax benefit to lower-income taxpayers who contribute to retirement accounts, a sort of bonus for saving money for later. The amount of your credit will be 10%, 20%, or 50% of your retirement contribution depending on your AGI (the limits change every year). These have to be new contributions, not rollovers, in order to qualify. You can't take this credit if you're under eighteen, a full-time student, or claimed as a dependent on someone else's tax return.

The credit is based on up to $2,000 of contributions for single filers and $4,000 for married filing jointly. That makes the maximum credit $1,000 for single filers and $2,000 for married filing jointly. To take advantage of the Saver's Credit, you have to complete IRS Form 8880 as part of your tax return. This credit is nonrefundable, so it can lower your tax bill to zero but not generate a tax refund.

EDUCATION CREDITS

There are two tax credits available to offset the costs of post-high school education: the American Opportunity Tax Credit (AOTC) and the Lifetime Learning Credit (LLC). Though each has its own set of rules, they do have five in common:

1. Qualified education expenses were paid for higher education.
2. An eligible student had to be enrolled at an eligible institution.
3. That eligible student is you, your spouse, your dependent child, or another dependent that you can claim on your taxes.
4. You can't claim the credit if your filing status is married filing separately.
5. You must file IRS Form 8863 with your tax return to claim the credit.

The AOTC is a partially refundable credit that can help you lower your tax bill by up to $2,500, and up to 40% of that may be refundable. To claim it you must have paid at least that much in qualified education expenses such as tuition, books, supplies, and mandatory fees (like lab fees) during the tax year. You get to claim 100% of the first $2,000 you spent and 25% of the next $2,000. The credit begins to phase out for single taxpayers with MAGI of $80,000 (or $160,000 for married filing jointly) and disappears if the MAGI exceeds $90,000 ($180,000 for married filing jointly).

This credit is available only for undergraduate students pursuing degrees or other credentials within their first four years of higher education and can only be claimed for four years. If you are the student and paid these expenses, you can claim the credit if no one else can claim you as a dependent. If you're the parent and paid the expenses for your child, you can only claim the credit if you can also claim the child as a dependent. If you did not directly pay the expenses, you cannot take this credit.

The LLC can be used for any kind of qualified higher education expenses, including those used to gain or improve job skills. This nonrefundable credit can reduce your tax bill by up to $2,000 per year, with no limit on the number of years it can be claimed. Unlike the AOTC, you don't have to be pursuing a degree to qualify for this credit—you can just be taking courses. The LLC covers expenses paid for tuition and fees required for enrollment.

You can claim both credits in the same tax year but not for the same student or the same expenses. The IRS offers an interactive app to help you figure out which education credit you qualify for. You can find that on their website at www.irs.gov.

USE TAX-ADVANTAGED ACCOUNTS

Pay Now or Pay Later

Tax-advantaged accounts offer special tax benefits like tax-free and tax-deferred income. Tax-free accounts are funded with money that's already been taxed (after-tax dollars), and the income and gains they produce won't be subject to income taxes. Tax-deferred accounts are funded with pre-tax dollars, and that money plus any earnings related to it won't be taxed until a later time, usually when the money is eventually withdrawn. Both types of tax benefits give your money more opportunity to grow than if you'd been paying taxes on their earnings all along.

On the flip side, these types of accounts generally restrict your access to your money, either based on your age or what you're using the money for. That's the trade-off for the tax benefits you get, and for many people the difference in growth will be worth the restrictions. These accounts also give you extra opportunities for tax planning now and for the future.

INDIVIDUAL RETIREMENT ACCOUNTS

Individual retirement accounts, better known as IRAs, were created in 1974 under the Employee Retirement Income Security Act (ERISA). They were introduced to help people who didn't have access to pensions to give them a tax-advantaged way to save for retirement. Contributions are tax deductible, reducing current taxable income and tax bills, to incentivize people to save. All earnings in the account grow tax-deferred, meaning there's no annual tax on those earnings, which helps speed up growth. When money is eventually withdrawn from the IRA, those withdrawals increase taxable income and are subject to regular income taxes.

These original IRAs are known as traditional IRAs, funded with pre-tax dollars of earned income (meaning income from employment). Because that money has never been taxed, account holders must start taking withdrawals called required minimum distributions (RMDs) when they reach a certain age (seventy-three as of 2024).

Spousal IRAs

You can only contribute to an IRA if you have earned income. Spousal IRAs allow working spouses make contributions on behalf of non-working spouses, as long as they're married and file a joint tax return. The non-working spouse is the sole owner of that IRA and all of the money in it.

You can use IRAs strategically to manage your tax bill. If you believe your current income tax rates are higher than they will be after you retire, it makes sense to reduce current taxable income. Making the maximum IRA contribution will lower your tax bill. The maximum contribution for 2024 is $7,000 plus an additional catch-up contribution of $1,000 for taxpayers over fifty. Contributions for any tax year must be made by the due date of the tax return including extensions; for example, you can make a 2024 IRA contribution any time before April 15, 2025, or if you filed a federal income tax extension before October 15, 2025.

ROTH IRAS

Roth IRAs work in the opposite way of traditional IRAs. The current contribution is made with after-tax dollars (no current tax deduction) and all the withdrawals are tax-free (as long as you follow the rules). That means all of the account earnings and growth will never be subject to income taxes. On top of that, since the original income was already taxed, Roth IRA owners are not required to take RMDs, allowing for more flexible budgeting after retirement. Since proper withdrawals are not included in taxable income, it's easier to qualify for income-capped tax deductions and tax credits, and it's less likely that Social Security benefits will be taxed. The catch: There are income caps to determine whether you can contribute to a Roth IRA.

WORKPLACE RETIREMENT PLANS

Many employers offer workplace retirement plans to help their employees save for retirement (and get some tax benefits for the employers themselves). In some of these plans, employees make contributions through payroll deductions. Other plans call for employer contributions on behalf of employees, and some allow for both types of contributions. Each plan comes with different contribution limits. These workplace retirement plans include 401(k) plans, 403(b) plans, 457 plans, employee stock ownership plans (ESOPs), Savings Incentive Match Plan for Employees (SIMPLE) IRA plans, pensions, and profit-sharing plans.

All of these plans offer tax benefits, including tax-deferred growth and earnings. Traditional versions of workplace retirement plans (including most of the ones listed in this section) provide current tax deductions for employee contributions. Employer contributions on behalf of employees are also tax-deferred. Roth versions of employer plans use post-tax money for employee contributions (meaning no current tax deduction), and all qualified withdrawals are tax-free. You can find out more about workplace retirement plans on the IRS website at www.irs.gov.

SELF-EMPLOYED RETIREMENT PLANS

Self-employed retirement plans are basically workplace retirement plans for people who are self-employed, giving them the opportunity to put away much more toward retirement than an IRA would allow. These plans are geared toward solopreneurs with no employees (though they can be used by other types of businesses too). The most common retirement plans among self-employed individuals include Solo 401(k) plans and Simplified Employee Pension IRAs (SEP-IRAs, or SEPs).

Solo 401(k) plans are set up for one participant only but otherwise work exactly the same as other 401(k) plans. As the employee, individuals can contribute the lesser of $23,000 (as of 2024) of their earned income or salary (if the business is set up as a corporation) from that job. Earned income here has a special calculation: total net profits for the year minus half of self-employment taxes and the plan contribution. As the employer, they can contribute up to 25% of their compensation or earned income. The maximum combined contribution (employee plus employer) is $69,000 (for 2024).

SEP-IRAs work a little differently. The business must set up a traditional IRA for each participant, and only the business makes the contributions. The most you can contribute to a SEP is 25% of earned income, up to $69,000 (for 2024). Earned income here has a special calculation: total net profits for the year less half of self-employment taxes and the plan contribution. If that sounds confusing, it is. The IRS provides a special worksheet for this calculation if you want to try to do it yourself, or you can turn to tax software programs or tax professionals that can figure out the contribution for you. Like regular IRAs, SEPs can be established and funded by the due date of the company's tax return, including extensions.

HEALTH SAVINGS ACCOUNTS

Health savings accounts (HSAs) are among the most underused and least understood tax-advantaged accounts. HSAs offer triple tax benefits to people who are eligible to participate:

- Pre-tax contributions (you pay less tax now)
- Tax-free growth (you don't pay tax on earnings as they happen)
- Tax-free distributions (when you use the funds for qualified medical expenses)

Plus, once you reach age sixty-five, you can use that money for non-medical reasons without getting hit with any tax penalties, though you will have to include the withdrawals in your taxable income and pay regular income tax on them. There are strict limits for eligibility that do keep many Americans from taking advantage of these beneficial accounts. HSAs are available only to people with high-deductible health plans (HDHPs).

TAX-SAVING STRATEGIES FOR RETIREMENT ACCOUNT WITHDRAWALS

Why Am I Still Paying Taxes?

For many retirees, keeping taxable income as low as possible is a crucial part of budgeting. That includes people who retire early (before the age of fifty-nine and a half), when they could be subject to early withdrawal penalties for pulling money out of tax-advantaged retirement accounts. With careful planning, you can manage your retirement tax situation, especially if you start making moves well ahead of time. This can give you more flexibility when it comes to minimizing taxable income and taxes in retirement. Even if you're not able to make sizable moves now, knowing which accounts to contribute to and in which order to take retirement distributions can help you reduce taxes (and potential tax penalties).

UNDERSTANDING RMDS

If you have any type of traditional retirement account (those funded with pre-tax dollars) like an IRA or a 401(k), you'll have to take required minimum distributions (RMDs) as soon as you turn age seventy-three. That means every year you *must* take at least the RMD out of your retirement account. The RMD will be added to your taxable income and subject to income taxes.

There's a set IRS formula to figure out each year's RMD: the value of each retirement account as of December 31 of the prior year divided by the appropriate life expectancy factor as published by the IRS (available at www.irs.gov). Though you have to calculate the RMD for each traditional retirement account separately, you may be able to withdraw the overall total from a single account. Married couples that both have traditional retirement accounts must each take their own RMDs (even if they file joint tax returns).

RMD Math

Here's an example of how to calculate your RMD. Suppose your only IRA had $200,000 in it on December 31 of last year, and you just turned seventy-three. According to the IRS Uniform Lifetime Table, your life expectancy factor is 26.5. For the RMD calculation, divide last year's ending balance of $200,000 by 26.5, which is $7,547.17. That's the minimum amount you must withdraw from your IRA.

The consequences for not taking the full RMD each year is severe. You have to pay a 25% excise tax on the amount not withdrawn. If you correct that and take the RMD within two years, that penalty drops down to 10%. These penalties were reduced down from 50% by the SECURE 2.0 Act. Avoid these penalties by taking the correct RMD every year.

QUALIFIED CHARITABLE DISTRIBUTIONS

Retired taxpayers at least seventy and a half years old who want to donate to charitable organizations have an extra tax-advantaged option called qualified charitable distributions (QCDs). With a

QCD, your donation gets transferred directly from your retirement account to the charity of your choice. That withdrawal does not get included in your AGI, resulting in lower taxable income. This can help you avoid owing taxes on Social Security benefits and increase your eligibility for certain tax deductions and credits. Plus, QCDs count toward your RMD, as long as you follow all the rules (see www .irs.gov).

Using a QCD works out better than if you take a withdrawal and then make a charitable donation. The withdrawal would increase your AGI and taxable income. You would have to itemize your deductions to claim the charitable contribution. If the contribution exceeds the annual IRS limit (60% of AGI for 2024), a portion would not be deductible for that year. You can sidestep all of these potential hassles with a QCD.

ROTH CONVERSIONS

As discussed previously, Roth IRAs offer a distinct tax advantage over other types of retirement accounts with tax-free withdrawals (as long as you follow all the rules) and no RMDs. But some taxpayers can't contribute to Roth IRAs because their AGI exceeds IRS limits of $161,000 for single taxpayers and $240,000 for married couples filing jointly (for 2024). Others have contributed to a traditional workplace retirement plan and did not have a Roth option. The solution is Roth conversions.

When you convert a traditional retirement account to a Roth IRA, you'll pay income taxes on the full amount of the conversion, which can make it difficult for some people to manage. The conversion amount gets added to your income, just as if you had taken a withdrawal. If you decide to make a Roth conversion, make sure you have enough cash available to pay the full tax bill that comes along with it.

Converting strategically over several years can make this more practical. In years where income is lower, you can convert more. You can also plan to convert only the amount that would keep you in the same tax bracket.

In some cases, conversions can be more complicated than expected, such as when a taxpayer has both pre-tax and post-tax money in their traditional IRAs. It's best to talk with a tax professional before doing a Roth conversion to make sure it's done in the most beneficial way. Done strategically and correctly, Roth conversions can significantly reduce your tax burden in retirement.

Be aware of the five-year rule here: You can't make withdrawals from converted Roth IRAs for five years. The IRS applies this rule to each Roth conversion separately. The clock starts on January 1 of the year you do the conversion, regardless of when it's actually done. So, for example, a Roth conversion done in November 2025 would start the five-year clock on January 1, 2025.

FUNDING AND TAPPING INTO NON-RETIREMENT ACCOUNTS

Not everyone wants to lock up their money in exchange for tax benefits, and even people who do should consider keeping at least a portion of their wealth in non-retirement accounts. The disadvantage here is the annual tax on all account earnings whether or not you withdraw them, but once they've been taxed they won't get taxed again. This tax-along-the-way system results in slower growth due to the tax drag. However, you can access your money at any time without paying hefty penalties to the IRS.

When you decide to sell off investments, you have more flexibility for managing the tax hit. You can decide on the timing of the sale, and when you do sell for a profit you're only taxed on the profit itself, and then based on the lower capital gains rates. In contrast, all taxable withdrawals from retirement accounts are taxed at income tax rates, plus with RMDs you have to pull out the money whether you want to or not. Also, there's no limit to how much money you can put into non-retirement savings and investment accounts (as opposed to strict caps on retirement account contributions) and you can make unrestricted withdrawals whenever you want.

TAX-SAVING STRATEGIES FOR INVESTMENTS

Scrooge McDucking It

All investments come with costs, from fees and expenses to commissions and taxes—including a few types of potential taxes. Investment earnings, like interest and dividends, are subject to income taxes. When investments are sold, they may be subject to capital gains taxes. Other types of taxes may kick in based on your income.

Understanding how taxes affect your investments ahead of time can help you plan more effectively, allowing you to use the tax laws to your advantage. Tax-efficient investing helps you keep more of your money and lose less of it to federal and state taxes, which can take a tremendous toll on your nest egg.

BUY AND HOLD VERSUS TRADING

While earnings on investments get taxed as they're earned, capital gains (or losses) only come into play when an investment is sold. Buy and hold investors (people who buy investments and hold on to them) tend to have fewer transactions than investor-traders, people who buy and sell investments quickly and frequently. Capital gains taxes favor buy and hold investors, as long-term capital gains are taxed at lower rates than short-term capital gains. For tax purposes, "long-term" refers to securities held for more than one year and "short-term" refers to securities held for one year or less.

Long-term capital gains tax rates range from 0% to 20% depending on your AGI, and the income thresholds change annually based on inflation. For example, single filers with long-term capital gains and an AGI less than $47,025 will pay no taxes on their gains (the 0% rate), but if their AGI was $120,000, they'd pay a 15% capital gains tax. Short-term capital gains are taxed at regular income tax rates, so tax rates on those gains would range from 10% to 37%. You can reduce investment taxes significantly by only selling investments that you've held for more than one year and taking advantage of the lower long-term capital gains rates.

Wash Sales

When an investor sells a security at a loss and buys that same security (or a substantially similar one) again within thirty days either before or after the sale date, the IRS classifies that as a wash sale. Capital losses from a wash sale cannot be used to offset capital gains for tax purposes. However, the loss does get added into the basis of the purchased security and can reduce future gains.

TAX LOSS HARVESTING

Tax loss harvesting is a common strategy used to offset capital gains with planned capital losses. Here's how it works. Toward the end of a year where you have a lot of taxable capital gains, you look through your investment portfolio for securities that aren't performing well and could be sold at a loss. You analyze those securities and decide which ones make the most sense to sell. The resulting losses can be used to offset your capital gains, thereby lowering or even eliminating capital gains taxes. If the losses end up exceeding the gains for a net loss overall, up to $3,000 of the capital loss can be written off against your other income.

This strategy can include all types of investments including stocks, bonds, mutual funds, and cryptocurrency (as of May 2024, the IRS considers crypto a capital asset rather than a currency). For example, if you have a large gain from selling stocks, you can offset that by selling cryptocurrency at a loss. You'll also want to avoid wash sales so as not to invalidate the tax loss harvesting strategy.

TAX-EFFICIENT INVESTING

Taxes can take a huge bite out of your investment returns, so many investors look for ways to minimize that with tax-efficient investing. The higher your tax bracket, the bigger effect this will have, potentially leading to significant tax savings annually.

The first main rule of thumb: Hold tax-efficient investments in taxable accounts that maximize their effects. Putting tax-efficient investments inside tax-exempt or tax-deferred accounts (like IRAs) erases their key tax benefits. Tax-efficient investing applies to investment earnings such as interest and dividends. It also applies to capital gains generated inside mutual funds, but not capital gains from selling your securities.

Examples of tax-efficient investment include:

- **Municipal bonds:** Interest is not subject to federal income tax and may also be exempt from state and local taxes.
- **US Treasury bonds:** Interest is not subject to state and local taxes.
- **Series I bonds:** Interest is not subject to state and local taxes.
- **Exchange-traded funds (ETFs) and index funds:** Capital gains are lower due to less internal turnover than managed funds.

All of these investments come with lower tax burdens than other types of investments, helping to lower your overall taxable investment income.

BE AWARE OF THE NIIT

The net investment income tax (NIIT) affects taxpayers with investment income and MAGI (modified adjusted gross income) over IRS limits. Investment-related income here includes interest and dividends, capital gains, royalties, rents, gains on sale of rental properties, and non-qualified annuities.

The income thresholds for the NIIT are $200,000 for single filers and heads of household, $250,000 for married couples filing jointly, and $125,000 for married filing separately. This 3.8% additional flat tax gets applied to the lesser of the net investment income or the excess of MAGI over the appropriate threshold.

Here's how the NIIT works: Say you're a head of household with $20,000 of net investment income and a MAGI of $225,000. Your MAGI is over the limit by $25,000 ($225,000 – $200,000). You'll owe the 3.8% tax on $20,000 net investment income because that's less than the $25,000 excess MAGI. Your extra tax would come to $760 (0.038 × $20,000). You can take steps to reduce or avoid the NIIT by strategically timing security sales or implementing tax loss harvesting, for example.

WATCH OUT FOR AMT

The alternative minimum tax (AMT) is the least amount of tax you can pay based on IRS rules. Designed to have wealthy people pay a fairer share of taxes, the AMT affects more people than ever. Basically, AMT figures out what your tax would be if you got fewer tax breaks and some of your tax-free income was taxable, which could result in a higher tax than originally calculated. The current AMT rules were put in place under the TCJA and will expire after 2025 unless Congress acts to extend them.

Two investment-related items may trigger the AMT: large capital gains and exercising employee stock options. Just because you end up owing AMT in one tax year doesn't mean you'll face it every year. With the TCJA's high exemptions and phase-out thresholds, it would take a big gain to put you over the edge. If you're coming close to being hit with AMT, some tax planning done before year-end (like tax loss harvesting) can help keep it from being triggered.

TAX-SAVING STRATEGIES FOR RENTAL INCOME

Sweet, Sweet Depreciation

Owning rental properties can offer significant tax benefits along with the potential for a lucrative source of positive cash flow. Profitable properties can generate taxable income, but there are legal ways to reduce that income and its tax effect. You can take deductions against rents and other income received, use the popular fourteen-day loophole, and take advantage of potential capital gains deferrals with an exclusive real estate strategy. The IRS has some very specific rules about rental real estate income, so it's best to work with a professional to take advantage of the benefits.

PASSIVE OR ACTIVE

The first thing to understand about rental income is that the IRS generally considers it to be passive activity income. That means you will pay tax on the net profits every year you have them but generally cannot deduct losses from your other income. It also means that your income here is considered investment income and potentially subject to the 3.8% NIIT.

However, if you can be classified as a real estate professional, that transforms the way losses can be applied. Real estate professionals, for tax purposes, include anyone who devotes at least half of their working hours to the rental business and more than 750 hours per year on this activity. Some examples of real estate professional duties include developing properties, construction, renovations, property acquisitions, and property management.

For example, if you spend time choosing and buying a rental property, fixing it up, and managing the property, you may qualify as a real estate professional. On the other hand, if you buy a rental property and hire out everything else, you probably won't. When you do qualify as a real estate professional, the income and losses generated by your rental properties are considered active income. That means any losses can be deducted against other income, lowering your taxable income and overall tax liability. It also means this income will not be considered investment income and won't be subject to the NIIT.

Active participation is another way you may be able to use at least a portion of rental losses against other income. The IRS allows active participants to deduct up to $25,000 of rental real estate activity losses as long as they meet the requirements and don't exceed income limits. To qualify for this special deduction, you must own at least 10% of the property and participate in making management decisions. This includes selecting new tenants, deciding terms of rental agreements, and approving spending for repairs and renovations. This deduction begins to phase out with MAGI over $100,000.

MAXIMIZE DEDUCTIONS

When you own rental property, you can deduct all of the expenses related to purchasing owning, managing, and maintaining the property. All of these can offset rental income, which can result in tax losses at the same time as positive rental cash flow (you're receiving more money than you're spending on the property during the year).

Some common deductible rental expenses include mortgage interest, property taxes, insurance, maintenance and repairs, management fees, advertising, home office expenses, utilities, and accounting and legal fees.

It's important to track the expenses carefully so you don't end up missing some and paying more taxes than you should. Active landlords may also be able to deduct mileage for trips to and from the property as long as they keep a mileage-tracking log. Along with these regular expenses, rental property owners can also deduct depreciation on the building (but never the land) and other assets (such as washing machines, sheds, and furniture).

Depreciation is an accounting and tax expense that spreads the cost of an asset over its entire useful life rather than taking the full cost as an expense all at once. Residential rental real estate has a useful life of twenty-seven and a half years according to the IRS and depreciates over that term.

THE FOURTEEN-DAY LOOPHOLE

There's a special tax loophole, sometimes called the "Augusta Rule" for taxpayers who rent out their homes for fourteen days or less during the year. Section 280A(g) of the tax code allows homeowners to rent out their personal residence for up to fourteen days per year without having to report the rental income on their tax returns. This strategy can be used for primary, secondary, and vacation homes that are otherwise only used as personal residences. For example, if you go away for one week over the summer and rent your house out to someone else while you're not there, that rental income does not have to be reported. Rent it out for fifteen days, though, and now you have taxable rental income.

There's a lot of misinformation floating around about this particular strategy, so be wary of advice you see on social media. For example, there are a lot of social posts suggesting you can rent your house to your small business for work events, take the deduction on the business side, and just pocket the income on the homeowner side. This strategy does not apply in all situations, and the rules for proper documentation and substantiation here are strict. So, make sure to talk to an experienced tax professional to ensure everything is done correctly; you don't want the IRS to overturn your position on an audit.

Birth of the Augusta Rule

Every year, the wealthy residents of Augusta, Georgia, would rent out their homes for a couple of weeks as people flocked to the city for the Masters golf tournament. In the 1970s, they lobbied heavily for a special tax exemption since their homes weren't really rental properties. They got their tax break in the form of IRC Section 280A(g).

1031 EXCHANGES

Normally when you sell property for a profit, you'll pay tax on those gains. But real estate comes with a special tax advantage called the Section 1031 exchange. It doesn't negate the taxes entirely but defers them indefinitely when you use this strategy correctly.

Also called a like-kind exchange, this move allows you to use the sale proceeds from the old property to purchase a similar property and transfer those gains to the new property. A like-kind property doesn't mean it has to be exactly the same, like a two-bedroom single family home for another two-bedroom single family home. Rather, the replacement property has to have the same character. For example, apartment buildings and office buildings would count as similar here. The basic idea is that you (the property owner) never receive any sale proceeds, so there isn't any income to tax currently.

The rules for this strategy are very specific and complex, so involving an experienced professional is a must. But there are some basic steps that need to be followed in every 1031 exchange.

1. Identify the rental property you want to sell.
2. Hire a qualified intermediary, an experienced professional that oversees the process and manages the money throughout the exchange.
3. Identify the like-kind property you want to buy.
4. Mind the two strict IRS deadlines: First, identify the replacement property in writing within forty-five days of the original sale. Second, purchase the replacement property within 180 days of the old property's sale date or your tax return due date, whichever is earlier.
5. Report the exchange to the IRS using Form 8824.

The most important part is choosing the right qualified intermediary, a legitimate professional with experience facilitating 1031 exchanges. This person cannot be a relative or any professional (like a lawyer or real estate agent) that you've worked with during the past two years. And without a proper intermediary, the exchange may be invalidated, erasing the tax benefits. You can learn more about Section 1031 exchanges in IRS Publication 544 on their website at www.irs.gov.

SAVING ON PROPERTY, SALES, AND ESTATE TAXES

Taxing at Every Turn

While income taxes can eat up a huge chunk of your money, property taxes and sales taxes can cost you thousands of dollars, even tens of thousands of dollars, every year. Gift and estate taxes can whittle down the inheritance you planned to leave for your family. Luckily, there are steps you can take to minimize all kinds of tax bites. The strategies differ based on type of tax, but there are ways to reduce each if you know how and plan ahead.

PROPERTY TAX SAVINGS STRATEGIES

Property taxes vary widely by state and locality, with effective rates ranging from 0.32% to 2.23% on the assessed value of your home. Some localities pile on to state property tax rates, making the annual expense even higher. On average, US homeowners pay around $2,400–$3,000 a year in property taxes.

Since property values tend to rise over time, property taxes increase regularly as well. And unlike mortgage payments, property tax payments never disappear (unless you no longer own the property). That's why it pays to do all you can to keep your property tax bill as low as possible.

The first thing you can do is to review your property tax records to make sure they're correct and reflect the current state of the property. The property value is based on an assessment, an estimated amount based on the market value of your home. This estimate includes the lot size, number of rooms, and square footage. Always let the assessor know if there are mistakes that could affect your home's value.

If everything looks correct but you feel your tax bill is higher than it should be, you can appeal it. In most cases, you'll need a lawyer to file the appeal for you for the cost of a filing fee. The tax assessor's office will review your appeal and make their decision, which can take months. If they find in your favor, they'll reduce your assessment, thereby lowering your property tax bill.

Renter's Credits

Renters don't pay property taxes directly, but their rent payments do go toward this expense. Many states offer tax credits to renters to help offset the indirect property taxes they pay. The credit often depends on your rent-to-income ratio, the percentage of your income that's used up by rent. Check your state's website to see if they offer this credit and how to apply.

You may also qualify for certain property tax rebates or exemptions if you or your property qualify in specific categories like senior, people with disabilities, veterans, certain farms and other agricultural properties, and homesteads. However, many of these have to be applied for specifically. You may, for example, have to file a homeowner's property tax credit application, apply for property tax relief, or complete a request for a homestead tax refund.

SALES TAX STRATEGIES

As of 2024, forty-five states and Washington, DC, collect sales taxes, and localities within thirty-eight states also charge sales taxes. State-level sales tax rates (among the states that have it) range from 2.9% in Colorado to 7.25% in California. In the first months of 2024 alone, state and local governments collected nearly $140 million in sales taxes. That works out to around half a billion dollars annually, and as prices increase, so do sales taxes. Unfortunately, there aren't many ways to reduce the amount of sales taxes you pay (other than buying less or less expensive items), but there are a few things you can do to lighten the load.

Take advantage of sales tax holidays, time periods designated by the state when eligible purchases become sales tax–free. These sales tax holidays can last anywhere from a single day to a couple of months, depending on the state. They're often themed, like back-to-school or energy-saving appliances. Arkansas, for example, hosts an annual sales tax–free weekend on certain clothing, accessories, school supplies, and electronics. Over twenty states have some kind of sales tax holiday on the books. You can find out whether your state or a neighboring state offers this by checking the states' websites. Also, if you're looking to buy a new car, you can trade in an old car to lower the sales price of the new one. This often drastically lowers the sales tax.

ESTATE AND GIFT TAX PLANNING

Whenever you give (not sell) someone an asset, it's considered a potentially taxable gift. Estate and gift taxes work together: Assets given during your lifetime count as gifts, and assets transferred at death count as part of your estate. All together, these assets transfers *could* add up to a huge tax bill, but the IRS rules allow for big exemptions that shield most Americans' assets from being taxed.

Every year people are allowed gift tax exemptions. For 2024, the annual exemption for gifts is $18,000 per giftee. (So, you can give $18,000 to as many people as you'd like.) Married couples can use a strategy called gift-splitting, which effectively doubles the exemption. Gifting strategically can help you avoid going over the annual exemption each year, keeping those gifts out of your eventual estate entirely.

Some gifts don't count toward the limit at all when you handle them properly. For example, if you pay someone else's tuition directly to the school, that payment isn't considered a gift. But, if you gave the student tuition money so they could pay the school themselves, it would go toward the annual gift exemption. It works the same way for medical expenses paid directly to providers. However, there's no limit on how much you can gift to your spouse.

You can also engage in estate planning to help stay below the lifetime limit ($13.61 million in 2024). Starting January 1, 2026, though, the generous estate and gift tax exemptions instituted under the Tax Cuts and Jobs Act of 2017 will no longer apply (unless Congress takes action). Those exemptions will roll back to pre-TCJA levels, making many more Americans subject to potential gift and estate taxes.

That said, people who took advantage of the higher exclusions between 2018 and 2025 will not be penalized when the 2026 changes kick in. Anything that was exempted will stay exempted and not added back into the total gift and estate value moving forward. If your total estate may fall into the taxable zone after the rollback, consider talking with a financial planner to help you figure out the best ways to minimize potential taxation. You may choose to accelerate asset transfers before the rule change to allow your heirs to keep more of your estate.

Chapter 6

Preparing Your Income Taxes

Does thinking about doing your taxes give you a headache? If so, you're not alone. With thousands of rules and calculations to get right, coming up with your taxable income and total income taxes can seem confusing. However, a good grasp on the basics can get you on the right track. Even if you hire someone else to do your taxes, it's important to understand your tax return. After all, you are ultimately responsible for the information included, and you're the one who will be dealing with the IRS if something goes wrong.

Having a big picture view will help with understanding your tax return. This chapter helps with anything from selecting the correct filing status to learning which income needs to be reported to knowing all of the tax deductions and credits you qualify for. Plus, if you do decide to tackle your taxes yourself, you'll need a deeper understanding of all the forms required and what must be included when you file. This chapter will get you moving in the right direction.

WHAT'S YOUR FILING STATUS?

How Many in Your Party?

Every year when you file your taxes, you have to choose your filing status. The choice you make will affect everything from your standard deduction to available tax credits to tax rates and can have a big impact on your final tax bill. (In other words, it's extremely important to understand and get this information right!)

There are five main filing statuses: single, married filing jointly, married filing separately, head of household, and qualifying surviving spouse. Each comes with its own standard deduction and tax tables, so choosing the right filing status can have a big impact on your overall tax bill.

SINGLE

If you're not married and no one (but you) depends on you for more than half of their financial support, you fall into the single filing category. Marital status is determined by whether you're married on the last day of the tax year. So even if you were married for most of the year, if you're not legally married (either by divorce or annulment) on December 31, you count as single for tax purposes. Also, there's no way to trick the system here. The IRS knows all the tricks—like getting divorced at the end of December and getting remarried in January, for example.

The standard deduction for single filers (for tax year 2024) is $14,600. Certain exemptions, tax credits, and deductions based on income limits may not be available for single filers. On the plus side, you won't face any tax liabilities based on someone else's income situation.

MARRIED FILING JOINTLY

If you're married as of the last day of the tax year, you have the option of filing a joint tax return with your spouse. All of your information goes on a single return instead of two, saving time and tax prep fees. In many cases, filing together can reduce your total taxes due, and that means you'll either owe less or get more back (depending on how much you've paid during the year).

There is one caveat: When you file a joint tax return with your spouse, you're each personally responsible for all taxes, penalties, and interest due. That's why it's important that both of you are involved in preparing the return and making sure any obligations get paid. When one spouse takes full control of the tax finances and the other doesn't really know what's going on with them, that spouse could end up on the hook with the IRS.

MARRIED FILING SEPARATELY

Another option for married couples is to file separate tax returns. This filing status is less commonly used because it often results in an overall higher tax bill. This is not the same as using the "single" filing status, as married individuals don't have that option. Couples need to agree on this strategy because what one spouse does here affects the other. For example, if one spouse itemizes, they must both do so. When they do itemize, they have to split the deductions and make sure none get doubled up.

When married couples do file separately, they may (in some cases) lose out on some important tax benefits such as: deducting student loan interest, taking the Earned Income Tax Credit (EITC), deducting child and dependent care expenses, taking education credits, and deducting the full amount of IRA contributions. On top of all that, filing separately reduces the standard deduction and can result in higher tax rates. It can also affect the taxability of Social Security benefit payments.

Filing Jointly versus Filing Separately

Generally speaking, married couples end up with better tax situations when they file jointly. But in some circumstances, it may be more beneficial for a married couple to file separate tax returns using the "married filing separately" status.

Situations where filing separately could provide a tax advantage include:

- One spouse had high medical expenses.
- One spouse has an income-based student loan repayment plan (and income is monitored on the tax return).
- There's a significant income disparity.

In some cases, one spouse may be worried about tax liability if filing jointly. For example, if one spouse refuses to file tax returns, the other can still use the married filing separately status and file their own return. If someone suspects their spouse of tax evasion or tax fraud, filing separate returns can protect the innocent spouse from the criminal behavior of the other.

Most tax software will calculate the return both ways to see which status will be more beneficial, so you can see what the different outcomes would be without having to go through the trouble of rerunning all the numbers on two separate returns. Even if the tax bill comes out lower one way, it may still be better to file the other way based on your unique situation—working with an experienced tax professional during these times can come in handy.

HEAD OF HOUSEHOLD

The rules for using the head of household (HOH) filing status are stricter than for the other options. This status can be used by people who aren't married, paid at least half the support for their home, and paid for at least one other related person for the tax year. To claim HOH status, you have to be the primary financial support for someone else.

According to the IRS, "not married" can be a gray area when filing as HOH. It generally means not legally married, but it also includes circumstances where a soon-to-be former spouse hasn't lived in your household for at least the last six months of the year, as long as it's a permanent absence. You have to pay more than half the cost of maintaining your household for the tax year with your own money (and not support from an ex or anyone else). You also have to have a qualifying dependent, usually a child, that's related to you. Here, "dependent" means they can be listed as a dependent on your tax return and not on their own or someone else's. Qualifying relatives may include your unmarried child (unless they're married and you can still claim them as a dependent on your tax return), a stepchild, a foster child, a sibling, a niece or nephew, a grandchild, your parent, a stepparent, or an in-law.

Additionally, you must provide more than half of that qualifying dependent's support for the tax year and they must have lived with you for more than half of the year. If you meet all of those requirements, you can use the beneficial HOH filing status. That gives you a bigger standard deduction and better tax brackets, resulting in less taxable income and lower tax rates.

Tie Goes to the Higher Income

If your qualifying child spends equal time with you and their other parent, the IRS sets the deciding factor for who can use the head of household filing status since only one of you can use it. According to the IRS tiebreaker rules, the person who has the higher adjusted gross income can file as HOH.

QUALIFYING SURVIVING SPOUSE

The qualifying surviving spouse status is the only one that's temporary, and it's allowed only for taxpayers who have recently lost their spouse and have dependent children living at home. For the first return—the one for the tax year during which the spouse died—married filing jointly status can be used. After that, a surviving spouse can use this special status for the next two years (as long as they haven't remarried).

A main factor here is the children: There must be a qualifying child living in the home to use this filing status. In addition, similar to head of household, the surviving spouse must pay more than half of the costs of supporting the household. This filing status lets you file as if you were married and filing a joint tax return, with a higher standard deduction and more beneficial tax rates.

WHAT INCOME NEEDS TO BE REPORTED?

Does This Go on My Tax Form?

When people ask if they have to report "X" kind of income, the answer is virtually always yes. Reportable income may include even some nontaxable income, though it won't be subject to income taxes. No matter where the income is from, no matter how much it is, it needs to be reported on your tax return. The IRS is very strict about this, and not reporting income can lead to audits and other consequences.

If your income is low enough, typically meaning lower than the standard deduction for your filing status, you *may* not need to file a tax return. However, if you have self-employment income or other types of income, you will need to report it and file a tax return even if you won't owe any income taxes.

WHAT COUNTS AS INCOME?

According to the IRS, income can be taxable or not taxable. It can come in forms other than money. It can be money you earned either actively or passively. It includes income from worldwide sources, not just income received in the US. In fact, even money earned illegally must be reported on your tax return.

For federal income tax purposes, any goods, property, and services received all count toward total income. So if you barter with someone, swapping goods or services, you may have to include the value of the goods or services you received. This generally applies to businesses, like trading electrical repairs for car maintenance or a haircut for a used laptop. It normally doesn't apply to things like swapping babysitting with other parents in your neighborhood, for example.

Babysitting money, on the other hand, does need to be reported if it tops $400 in a single year. Anyone who babysits, walks dogs, mows lawns, or shovels snow and makes at least $400 (from all of their money-making activities) technically has to report it and file a tax return.

Bottom line: Unless it's specifically considered nontaxable or tax-exempt by statute, the income is taxable and has to be reported on your tax return.

Constructive Receipt

If you effectively receive income, even if you don't actually have the money, it counts as income to the IRS. For example, if you get a check for work you performed but don't cash it by year-end, it still counts as income in the year of receipt. If you divert a portion of your income to someone else, such as paying child support directly from your paycheck to your ex, that's still your income to report.

EARNED INCOME

Earned income comes from any kind of employment, whether you work for yourself or someone else. The classification matters for tax purposes because certain tax credits, like the Earned Income Tax Credit (EITC), are only available to people with earned income. Also, Social Security retirement benefits may be taxed when earned income exceeds certain thresholds.

Earned income as a whole includes salary and wages, self-employment income, bonuses, commissions, tips, and long-term disability benefits (in some cases). Earned income gets taxed differently than unearned income and is generally subject to payroll taxes (Social Security and Medicare).

INCOME FROM PASSIVE SOURCES AND PASSIVE ACTIVITY INCOME

Though income from passive sources and passive income seem like the same thing, the IRS considers them different. Income from passive sources does include passive activity income, but not all of it counts as passive activity income for tax purposes. All of it refers to money you bring in with little or no effort. To the IRS, income from passive sources includes everything that doesn't fall under the earned income umbrella.

Income from passive sources can be many things. Some examples are dividends, interest, capital gains (and losses), rents, royalties (not derived from work you produced), Social Security retirement benefits, pensions, and annuities.

Income from these sources get reported on your tax return. Some of them get taxed at your income tax rates, and special rates may apply to others. Losses from these sources get treated differently than earned income losses (like small business losses). For example, while the full amount of self-employment losses offsets other income, only $3,000 of net capital losses can be deducted against other income.

Passive activities, according to the IRS, include business activities you don't materially participate in (like being a silent partner) and rental real estate activities (unless you're a real estate professional). Generally, you cannot deduct net passive activity losses against other income except in specific circumstances.

NONTAXABLE INCOME

For federal (and often state) tax purposes, some kinds of income aren't taxable. In many cases these would not show up on your tax return, though sometimes they get reported but not included. Sources of nontaxable income are inheritance, life insurance proceeds (to the beneficiary), gifts, insurance reimbursements, workers compensation benefits, Supplemental Security Income (SSI), municipal bond interest, qualified withdrawals from Roth IRA or Roth 401(k) accounts, alimony (for divorces finalized after 2018), and child support.

Other forms of income may not be taxable depending on your specific situation. If you're unsure whether income you've received is taxable or must be reported on your tax return, consult with a tax professional.

INTERACTIVE TAX ASSISTANT

The IRS provides a tool on their website (www.irs.gov) called the Interactive Tax Assistant (ITA). It serves up answers to many tax questions based on your specific inputs about your circumstances. The tool can help you figure out a variety of tax-related things, including whether you have to report certain items of income.

For example, you can find out whether you have to report things like scholarships or fellowships, gambling winnings and losses, unemployment payments, fees received as the executor of an estate, and prizes or awards. Plus, you can use the ITA as many times as you want for as many questions as you have. On average, the inputs for each question take about three to five minutes to enter.

WHY ADJUSTED GROSS INCOME MATTERS

This Number Is Everything

One of the most important calculations on your tax return is adjusted gross income, or AGI. Along with being the starting point for your tax calculations, AGI plays a role in determining your eligibility for many tax deductions and credits. Most people pay more attention to their taxable income than to their AGI, but AGI is a key factor in getting to taxable income, affecting it more than you might realize. Some states use this number as the basis for your state taxable income, for example. Tax software will take care of the math for you, but it's important to know what goes into AGI so you can keep yours as low as possible. With strategic tax planning throughout the year, you may be able to use these adjustments to reduce your AGI, your taxable income, and your total tax.

HOW TO CALCULATE AGI

Calculating AGI is pretty straightforward. It starts with your taxable income and then subtracts certain "adjustments to income." First, you add up all of your taxable income from all sources (jobs, investments, business profits, pensions, etc.). Then you subtract all applicable adjustments for that tax year. Those adjustments get listed on Schedule 1, Part II in your tax return.

Common adjustments to income include self-employed health insurance premiums paid, half of your self-employment taxes, contributions made to self-employed retirement plans (like SEPs), contributions to a traditional IRA, educator expenses, contributions to a health savings account (HSA), student loan interest, moving expenses for members of the Armed Forces, and alimony payments for divorces prior to 2019. There are several other adjustments available, such as certain reforestation expenses and contributions by specific chaplains to retirement plans, but those are much less common. Be aware that "adjustments to income" do change from time to time, so an item you can deduct to reduce your AGI in one tax year may not be available in another.

Here's what AGI math looks like for your tax return. Let's say you have $50,000 of income from a job, $3,000 from a side gig, and $150 from interest and investment income. Your total gross income would be $53,150. Your adjustments include a $2,000 traditional IRA contribution and $2,500 of student loan interest, totaling $4,500. Your AGI would work out to $48,650 ($53,150 – $4,500).

HOW AGI AFFECTS YOUR TAXES

Several calculations in a typical tax return are based on your AGI. It's the deciding factor in whether you'll be eligible to take certain deductions or tax credits. You'll see that adjusted gross income appears on many different tax forms, not just your main Form 1040.

Your AGI determines whether or not you'll be able to deduct medical expenses, as the total paid for the year has to clear a hurdle of 7.5% of your AGI before you can deduct anything. Casualty losses must exceed 10% of AGI (plus $100) to be deductible. For these types of deductions, lower AGI means a bigger tax break. On the other side, you can only deduct charitable contributions up to 60% of AGI, so a higher AGI gets you a bigger tax deduction. These percentages may change from year to year, but they'll still be based on a percentage of AGI.

Eligibility for some tax credits, such as the Earned Income Tax Credit (EITC) and the Saver's Credit, is also based on AGI. Unlike deductions that use AGI percentages, tax credits are often available only to taxpayers with AGI below a certain limit. For example, you can't take the Saver's Credit if your AGI exceeds $38,250 for single filers or $76,500 for married filing jointly (for tax year 2024).

AGI AFFECTS MORE THAN TAXES

It's not only the IRS that pays attention to your AGI. Many other institutions use it as well, especially when determining your eligibility for certain income-based programs. Other times your AGI may come into play include applying for an income-driven student loan repayment plan, getting a loan (especially a mortgage), renting an apartment, verifying identity (typically on government websites), applying for health insurance in the Marketplace, obtaining car insurance, and applying for financial aid with the Free Application for Federal Student Aid (FAFSA). While in many of these situations you'll be asked for additional information, they often use AGI as a starting point to determine whether to proceed.

MODIFIED ADJUSTED GROSS INCOME (MAGI)

Modified adjusted gross income, or MAGI, is an offshoot of AGI that's used in different eligibility and tax calculations. For most people, it will be very close to or the same as their AGI. And unlike

AGI, this number won't appear anywhere on your tax return, but it may still affect your taxes.

MAGI affects whether you can make a tax-deductible contribution to a traditional IRA and whether you can contribute at all to a Roth IRA. It also determines if you'll be able to take advantage of the Premium Tax Credit when you purchase health insurance through the Marketplace. MAGI also affects eligibility for education credits, both the American Opportunity Tax Credit and the Lifetime Learning Credit. Additionally, MAGI comes into play if you're applying for certain benefits, including Medicaid and the Children's Health Insurance Program (CHIP).

AGI by the Numbers

According to the IRS, the average AGI in the US for the 2021 filing year (the most recent currently available in May 2024) was $76,539. But taking a closer look, that number varies widely by state. For example, the average AGI in Massachusetts was $101,863, while the average in Mississippi was $50,876.

To calculate MAGI, you start with AGI and add back some of the deductions. What you add back sometimes depends on the type of tax benefit involved. For example, for education credits there are different add backs than there are for IRA contributions. Other times, you'd add back things like untaxed foreign income, tax-exempt interest, and nontaxable Social Security benefits. Your tax professional or tax software will do all the calculations here.

STANDARD VERSUS ITEMIZED DEDUCTIONS

Everyone's Doing It

Deductions reduce your taxable income and your tax bill, so it's in your best financial interest to maximize those deductions as much as you can (legally, of course). You have two main options here: standard and itemized. The standard deduction is the same for everyone in the same filing status category. Itemized deductions are personal and can vary greatly.

Before the Tax Cuts and Jobs Act (TCJA) substantially increased the standard deduction, many more people itemized to put a bigger dent in their tax bills. The TCJA granted the highest ever standard deductions, limiting the number of taxpayers who would benefit from itemizing. When you're trying to figure out which to use, the answer is whichever gives you the bigger deduction—unless, that is, you're prohibited from using one or the other.

A LITTLE BACKGROUND

In 1944, Congress decided to make tax filing easier and introduced the standard deduction. It made processing the returns easier, as dealing with itemized deductions and receipts for millions of taxpayers was causing backlogs at the IRS. Now, taxpayers could simply deduct 10% of their taxable income to cover basic living expenses, and just pay tax on the rest.

That percentage lasted for twenty years, when lawmakers changed it to a fixed amount. The purpose of this change was to remove low-income citizens from the tax rolls. This way, anyone who made up to that standard deduction amount wouldn't have to file, and the IRS would have fewer returns to process. Over time the standard deduction has increased, sometimes by inches and other times by giant leaps. The biggest increase came courtesy of the TCJA, almost doubling the standard deduction and greatly reducing the number of taxpayers that itemized.

STANDARD DEDUCTION BASICS

The standard deduction is a fixed dollar amount that every taxpayer can use to reduce their taxable income. The amount depends on filing status, age, and whether or not you're blind. These numbers typically change every year, adjusted for inflation.

The three categories based on filing status include: single filers and married filing separately; married filing jointly; and head of household. The first group has the lowest standard deduction, the second group has the highest, and head of household falls in the middle. There's an extra $1,950 if you're over sixty-five or blind, and $3,900 if you're over sixty-five *and* blind.

If someone else (like your parents) can claim you as a dependent on their tax return, your standard deduction becomes whichever is greater: $1,300 or your earned income plus $450.

Every year, the IRS updates the standard deduction, but the amount tends to stay consistent. A big jump occurred with the passage of the TCJA in 2017, which almost doubled the amount from the prior year. Since then, the standard deduction has increased gradually every year. For the 2024 tax year, the standard deduction increased to:

- Single and married filing separately: $14,600
- Married filing jointly: $29,200
- Head of household: $21,900

These high standard deduction levels will expire on December 31, 2025 unless Congress acts before then to extend them.

THE INS AND OUTS OF ITEMIZING

The tax code allows you to deduct certain living expenses from your taxable income to reduce your tax burden. These itemized deductions, meaning you have to list them all individually and be able to prove they're legit, get reported on Schedule A as part of your tax return. Generally, you'd only itemize your deductions if they'd end up giving you a bigger tax break than the standard deduction, so many people don't bother with them. According to the IRS, since the TCJA, only around 11% of taxpayers itemize.

Some taxpayers are required to itemize their deductions. For example, if you and your spouse are using the married filing separately filing status and your spouse itemizes, you have to as well. Some nonresident and dual status aliens have to itemize too.

In some cases, however, it just pays to itemize. Allowable itemized deductions include medical expenses in excess of 7.5% of your AGI; state and local taxes (SALT), such as property and state income taxes, up to $10,000; home mortgage interest; charitable donations; casualty and theft losses; "other" itemized donations (including gambling losses to the extent of gambling winnings and impairment-related work expenses for a disabled person, for example).

As you'd expect, each of these comes with its own set of rules and limitations, but that doesn't mean you need to be worried about itemizing if the math works out better for you. Tax professionals and tax software know all the rules and can help make sure you don't deduct something that's not allowed. These deductions get listed on Schedule A as part of Form 1040.

THE BUNCHING DEDUCTIONS STRATEGY

When your total deductible expenses come close to the standard deduction, you can use a strategy called bunching to push them over the top. This allows you to get a bigger tax benefit for the current year and switch back to the standard deduction in the next tax year. Conversely, if you know you have a big expense coming up (like surgery or a major charitable donation) next year, you could use the same strategy with different timing.

For example, say you have higher-than-usual medical expenses one year, and they're enough to make itemizing worthwhile even though you would normally take the standard deduction. To make the most of your itemized deductions, you can cram more deductible expenses into the current tax year. That will increase the value of itemizing, further reducing your tax bill. In this situation, you could make an extra mortgage payment, pay for additional medical expenses like new glasses or a dentist appointment, or accelerate charitable donations (to individual organizations or through a donor-advised fund).

This strategy allows you to take advantage of greater itemized deductions in a year that you're able to itemize, maximizing the benefits and reducing your tax bill further.

TAXABLE INCOME AND TAX PAYMENTS

Add It Up, Subtract It Out

Your taxable income includes everything you earned or received during the year minus all of your allowable deductions. You use this figure to calculate your tax bill, which is also based on your filing status. From that total tax, you get to subtract any payments you've already made and any tax credits you're able to take. This may sound simple, but these calculations can actually get a little tricky depending on your tax situation. Even what seem like easy tax returns can quickly become complicated when you have multiple types of income or as you begin to claim credits and deductions. Reporting everything in the right place will ensure you're paying just the right amount of taxes.

REPORTING YOUR INCOME

Different types of income get reported in different places on the tax return. Some go straight onto Form 1040, while others get reported on other forms and schedules that carry forward to that main form. It's important to report your income in the right places so you end up paying the correct amount of tax on that income. Here's an overview of where the most common types of income go:

- Salary and wages (from Forms W-2): Form 1040
- Interest income (from Forms 1099-INT): Schedule B
- Dividend income (from Forms 1099-DIV): Schedule B

- Self-employment or small business income (or losses) for sole proprietors: Schedule C
- Capital gains or losses (from Forms 1099-B and 1099-DIV): Schedule D
- Rental income or losses: Schedule E, page one
- Income or losses from S corporations and partnerships (from Schedules K-1): Schedule E, page two

Some of these forms, like Schedule B, feed directly to Form 1040. Others, like Schedule C, transfer to Schedule 1 before finally showing up on the 1040. All of it comes together to calculate your total income.

ACCOUNT FOR ALL OF YOUR DEDUCTIONS

Both above-the-line and below-the-line deductions serve to reduce your taxable income. Since above-the-line deductions reduce your AGI (adjusted gross income) first, which can increase the dollar amount of other deductions, make sure to take every one you qualify for. Above-the-line deductions, also called adjustments to income, may include traditional IRA and HSA contributions, student loan interest, and educator expenses. These deductions go on Part II of Schedule 1 in your tax return, and the total flows up to the Form 1040. That total gets deducted from your total income to arrive at AGI.

Next comes either the standard deduction or itemized deductions. Any taxpayer can use the standard deduction, which is based on filing status. Taxpayers who have higher expenses can choose to itemize their deductions on Schedule A. Common itemized deductions include medical expenses, mortgage interest, state and local taxes (like income, property, and sales taxes) up to $10,000, and charitable contributions. Whichever method you choose, that total deduction gets taken from AGI to get to your taxable income. That figure is then used to calculate your tax, based on your filing status and tax bracket.

TAX AND CREDITS

Page two of Form 1040 focuses on tax calculations, including applicable credits and payments, to get to the bottom line: how much you owe or how much you'll get back. It starts with the tax calculated based on your taxable income, your filing status, and the applicable tax rates based on both your tax bracket and type of income. Tax software will do the math, but you could also run the calculations yourself if you have a solid working knowledge of the underlying principles.

Any additional taxes from Schedule 2 will flow to this tax section of the 1040. These additional taxes may include alternative minimum tax (AMT), self-employment tax, additional Medicare tax, household employment taxes (a nanny, for example), or net investment income tax (NIIT). There's a two-page list of potential additional taxes, but these are the most common. These get added to the calculated income taxes for a new total.

Next, this section applies nonrefundable tax credits, which are credits that can reduce your tax bill to zero but not below. These include the Child Tax Credit, the Credit for Other Dependents, and additional nonrefundable tax credits from Schedule 3. Those other credits include things like the Foreign Tax Credit, the Child and Dependent Care Credit, the Adoption Credit, and the Residential

Clean Energy Credit. The total nonrefundable taxes get subtracted from the tax calculated earlier, resulting in that year's total tax bill.

TAX PAYMENTS

During the last tax year, you probably made payments toward your eventual tax bill. (If you haven't, don't worry, but plan to do it this year.) There are basically three ways to do that: through withholding from a paycheck or other income source, estimated tax payments, and prior years' tax refunds applied to this tax year. Refundable tax credits—credits that can result in you getting extra money back— also count like tax payments here.

Some common refundable tax credits include the Additional Child Tax Credit, Earned Income Tax Credit, and American Opportunity Tax Credit. Additionally, page two of Schedule 3 details additional payments and credits. Those could include overpayment of Social Security taxes, the amount paid along with a request for extension, or the Premium Tax Credit (PTC). The total of these flows to the Form 1040 in the payment section.

Tax Return versus Tax Refund

Though people use the terms "tax return" and "tax refund" interchangeably, they're not the same thing. Your tax return is the document you file with the IRS detailing your income and deductions for the tax year. Your tax refund is the money you get back because you paid too much in taxes during the year.

All of these payments and refundable credits get totaled. That total gets deducted from your total tax. If the result is positive, you owe more money. If the result is negative, you're due a refund.

COMMON FORMS YOU'LL NEED

Is There a Form for That?

Every tax return starts with a version of IRS Form 1040. But most people's tax returns don't end there. Your return could include dozens of additional forms (some called schedules) depending on your total tax picture. In fact, even a "simple" tax return could run twenty pages long! While there are literally dozens of forms that could be included in a tax return, here we're just going to cover the most commonly used. You can find information about all tax forms on the IRS website at www.irs.gov.

There are two types of schedules: summary and detail. Schedules 1, 2, and 3 are summary forms that consolidate information from other forms included in the tax return. Other forms, including Schedules A through E, contain details about a particular type of income, deduction, or credit.

SCHEDULES 1, 2, AND 3

Congress has added three new schedules to contain all of the information on the tax form. Not everyone will use all of these schedules, but many taxpayers will need to include them in their tax packets.

The three schedules have different aspects to them. Schedule 1 includes additional income (like self-employment or rental income) and above-the-line deductions (like traditional IRA contributions). Schedule 2 includes additional taxes (like self-employment taxes). Schedule 3 includes additional credits (like the Child Tax Credit) and tax payments you've made other than through withholding. All three of these schedules collect information from other forms and then send it up to the Form 1040, which now acts like sort of a summary of your tax picture.

SCHEDULES A, B, C, D, AND E

In addition to Schedules 1–3, there are also commonly used schedules labeled alphabetically A–E. While Schedule A is used to report itemized deductions, the other schedules in this group report the details of different types of income. Some people will use all five of these schedules, others might use one or two, and some tax returns won't include any of them.

Schedule A

You'll use Schedule A when you want to itemize your deductions. Itemized deductions include medical expenses in excess of 7.5% of your AGI (adjusted gross income); state and local taxes (SALT) up to the $10,000 cap ($5,000 if married filing separately); charitable donations up to 60% of your AGI; and mortgage interest.

It makes sense to itemize your deductions when they total more than the standard deduction. In some cases, people itemize even when the standard deduction is greater due to things like state tax benefits from itemizing.

Schedule B

Schedule B is where you'll report interest and dividend income. Interest income typically comes from sources like savings accounts, certificates of deposit (CDs), and bonds. Dividends come from stock investments and some mutual funds. You have to pay tax on your interest and dividend income whether or not you withdraw the money.

Even if you earned taxable interest and dividends, you may not have to file Schedule B with your tax return. It's only required if you earned more than $1,500 in either interest or dividends, if you had signature power over a foreign account, and some other less common scenarios (like earning interest from a seller-financed mortgage or earning accrued interest on bonds).

Schedule B has three parts. Part I is to report taxable interest earned, normally reported to you on Form 1099-INT. Part II is used to report ordinary dividends, usually reported to you on Form 1099-DIV. In those two sections, you'll provide an itemized list of the payers (like the name of the bank) and the amount received. If either of those sections reports income of more than $1,500, you have to complete Part III. Part III is used to report more than $1,500 in taxable interest or ordinary dividends; whether you had a foreign account; or if you received a distribution from or were a party to a foreign trust.

When you do need to file Schedule B, the information on it will flow up to your Form 1040, and you'll include the schedule when you file your complete tax return.

Schedule C

If you're self-employed or own a small business as a sole proprietor, your business income will get reported on Schedule C. This form acts sort of like a Profit and Loss Statement (P&L) with details about revenues, costs, and expenses to get to your taxable bottom line. As these forms are slightly outdated, they don't specifically include more current business expenses (like Internet) but they do list some common business expenses. Any expenses that don't fit into the IRS form boxes can get lumped into the "other" category and listed there.

The bottom line is your business's net profit (or loss)—the amount you'll be taxed on. It's also used in some other tax calculations, like any self-employment taxes due and the qualified business income (QBI) deduction (available through tax year 2025). For income tax purposes, your net income will flow to Schedule 1, and from there to Form 1040.

The Qualified Business Income Deduction

Thanks to the TCJA of 2017, pass-through business owners (including Schedule C businesses) may be able to deduct 20% of their net business profits from their taxable income. There are tons of rules and qualifications (like income limits) to take the QBI deduction. But many small business owners will qualify for these huge income tax savings.

Schedule D

Taxpayers use Schedule D to report gains and losses from selling capital assets as part of their complete tax returns. Capital assets include things like stocks, bonds, mutual funds, cryptocurrency, and real estate (like homes). This form splits these gains and losses into two types: short-term and long-term. Short-term includes any assets held for less than one year before being sold and are taxed at ordinary income tax rates. Long-term includes any assets held for one year or more before being sold and are taxed at special lower capital gains tax rates.

Capital losses, when you sell something for less than you paid for it, get subtracted from capital gains. When capital losses exceed capital gains, up to $3,000 worth can be used to offset other income in the current tax year (any remaining losses can be carried forward to future tax years). Whether you end up with net capital gains or losses, that number will flow up to your Form 1040 as part of your taxable income.

Schedule E

Schedule E, Supplemental Income and Loss, includes a few kinds of income. Part I focuses on rental income from properties you own or royalties you receive. Part II is where you list income from partnerships and S corporations, both of which are considered pass-through entities for income tax purposes. Part III is for income received from estates or trusts, and Part IV is for reporting income from Real Estate Mortgage Investment Conduits (REMICs), which won't be used by most people. The final section, Part V, summarizes the total income or loss, with a special section for real estate professionals.

Part I, Income or Loss from Rental Real Estate or Royalties, includes information about each specific property (for rentals) including the physical address, the number of days it was actually rented, and the number of days it was used for personal reasons. The next section in Part I asks for the type of property, such as single-family home or multi-family residence, or royalty. The remaining sections of Part I include the revenues and expenses for each property, and the profit or loss for each.

Part II, Income or Loss from Partnerships and S corporations, is where you list income that has been reported to you on Schedule K-1. It separates passive from nonpassive income, which are treated differently for tax purposes. Part III looks very similar to Part II, only it covers K-1 reporting from estates and trusts.

All of this information flows up to Schedule 1 and then to your Form 1040 as part of your taxable income.

TAXES AFTER RETIREMENT

I Still Have to Pay Taxes?

Most people expect their taxes will be lower in retirement because they'll have less income, and for the most part they're right. While most people will have taxable income post-retirement, you can take steps to minimize that or even avoid it entirely with some careful planning. At the same time, it's important to understand all the rules about retirement income or you could end up paying extra taxes and big tax penalties.

In retirement, your income was generally expected to be made up of Social Security benefits, pensions, and withdrawals from retirement accounts. That's not always how things work anymore, as many seniors work well into their "retirement" years. The types of income you have can affect how much tax you'll pay.

FORM 1040-SR

Once you turn sixty-five, you can take advantage of a special tax form for seniors called Form 1040-SR. It's similar to a regular 1040 in that it summarizes your taxable income, deductions, and credits for the year and results in either a balance due or a refund. The differences include larger, easier-to-read font and more prominence to issues that are more common for senior taxpayers.

For example, after age sixty-five, you're entitled to an additional standard deduction of $1,950 for single seniors (as of 2024) and $1,550 for married seniors. So for 2024, a single filer over sixty-five would get the $14,600 regular standard deduction plus the extra

$1,950 senior bump for a total standard deduction of $16,550. That section is emphasized on the 1040-SR.

PRE-TAX RETIREMENT ACCOUNTS AND RMDS

If you have pre-tax retirement accounts like traditional IRAs and 401(k)s, the money in those accounts hasn't been taxed yet. That's a huge source of potential revenue for the federal government, and they really want that tax revenue. That's where required minimum distributions (RMDs) come into play. RMDs were created to force people to withdraw funds from their pre-tax retirement accounts whether they needed the money or not. You can always take more than the RMD if you need it, but you can't take less without facing IRS penalties equal to 25% of the amount you were supposed to withdraw.

There have been a lot of changes to RMDs over the years, mainly focusing on when you have to start taking them and what happens if you don't. The most recent changes came in the SECURE 2.0 Act, which increased the start age to seventy-three in 2023 and to seventy-five in 2033. The Act also decreased the skipped withdrawal penalty from 50% to 25%, and if you correct the issue quickly, the penalty could be dropped to 10%.

Your RMDs will increase your taxable income and possibly your income tax bill. It's important to calculate them correctly and withdraw them correctly each year to avoid IRS issues. The calculation involves your age, your account balance, and your life expectancy (and, in some cases, your beneficiaries' life expectancies). The RMD is typically calculated by dividing the balance of each of your traditional retirement accounts (as of December 31 the prior year) by the IRS life expectancy factor from their published tables. You have to calculate each RMD separately if you have multiple accounts, but if you have more than one of the same type of account (like three IRAs, for example), you can take the withdrawals from one (or more) of them. However, if you have an IRA and a 401(k), you have to calculate and withdraw those RMDs separately. You can find out more about RMDs on the IRS website at www.irs.gov.

THE TAX BENEFITS OF ROTH IRAS

If you're able to contribute to or move money into a Roth IRA or Roth 401(k) plan, you'll be in a better tax position during retirement because withdrawals are tax-free (if you follow the rules), and they don't get included in your taxable income. Plus, there are no RMDs, so you don't have to withdraw money if you don't want to (for Roth 401(k) accounts the no-RMD rule begins in 2024).

Although you can always withdraw your contributions at any time with no tax hit, there are two important rules for tax-free earnings withdrawals: You must be at least fifty-nine and a half years old *and* the account has to have been open for at least five years. Once you meet both requirements, every penny of every withdrawal is completely tax-free.

Having access to tax-free income can also help minimize other income taxes in retirement. For example, Social Security benefits can be taxable if your income hits a certain level. Roth withdrawals can help you avoid that.

WHEN SOCIAL SECURITY BENEFITS ARE TAXABLE

Many people are shocked to find out that Social Security benefits are often subject to income taxes. If you file as single and your "combined income" is between $25,000 and $34,000 (for 2024), or married filing jointly with income between $32,000 and $44,000, 50% of your benefits will be taxable. If your total "combined income" exceeds $34,000 for single filers and $44,000 for married filing jointly, 85% of your retirement benefits will be taxable.

"Combined income" has a very specific definition here; it is a Social Security formula that equals your adjusted gross income (AGI) plus any nontaxable interest plus half of your Social Security benefits. According to the Social Security Administration (SSA), around 40% of people receiving benefits pay tax on them. When you consider that the average annual retirement benefit is $22,884 (so half would be $11,442), you can see that it doesn't take much to hit the lowest combined income level.

Tax Guide for Seniors

The IRS offers Publication 554, *Tax Guide for Seniors*, to help retirees navigate their yearly income tax returns. This surprisingly handy booklet helps seniors figure out their taxable and nontaxable income and tax credits, and whether they need to make estimated tax payments. It also contains worksheets that can help you calculate your likely tax bill so you can be better prepared come tax time.

TAX PREP OPTIONS

Pick Your Own Adventure

When it comes to preparing your annual income tax returns, you have two main options: Do it yourself or pay someone to do it for you. Once you've figured out which will work better for you and your tax situation, you'll have more choices to make.

For basic tax returns, DIY options can get the job done. But if your tax return includes a lot of schedules that you're not familiar with, hiring a professional can mean the difference between getting it right and getting a notice from the IRS.

USING FREE FILE

The IRS offers access to Free File tax software that's actually free to qualifying taxpayers. The agency has been wanting to bring this service fully in-house for years, and thanks to funding from the Inflation Reduction Act, the IRS was able to launch a twelve-state pilot Direct File program. Once all the kinks are worked out, the program will go nationwide. And in the meantime, taxpayers can go through the IRS website to access the IRS Free File options (if they qualify) and free fillable forms (anyone can use these).

For now, most people using Free File will be connected with an IRS partner. Those companies include 1040.com, FileYourTaxes.com, TaxAct, and TaxSlayer. Use the free IRS lookup tool, "Find Your Trusted Partner," to figure out which provider would be best for your situation.

People with AGI of $79,000 or less (regardless of filing status) qualify to use IRS Free File. Some of the individual providers may place additional restrictions on filers, such as age limits or lower income limits. In addition, not all providers offer state filing as part of the same free deal. Some states offer their own versions of free filing, so you can check your state's tax website for that.

PAYING FOR TAX SOFTWARE

If you don't qualify for Free File or you need more sophisticated tax software options, you can use paid tax software. There are a lot of options out there, and they all offer a variety of packages for different types of taxpayers. Knowing what you need ahead of time will help you save add-on fees if you end up needing more forms than the package provides. Some also charge additional fees for state returns, especially if you need to file in more than one state. And be wary of their "free" options, which typically include only the most basic tax returns with additional charges for anything else. Add-ons may include itemized deductions, self-employment income, and distributions (money you took out) from an HSA or a retirement account.

Other than that, choose whichever reliable provider is the easiest for you to use. The tax laws are the same no matter which software you use. The differences are mainly in how you enter the information and interact with the software.

DO YOU NEED A TAX PROFESSIONAL?

There are many circumstances where it makes sense to hire a tax professional, even though that *seems* to be the more expensive option. In fact, working with an experienced tax professional can end up saving you money, especially over time, as they can help you with tax planning strategies. While most tax software options come with walk-throughs, chat or phone help, and "audit checks," they can't manage information they don't have. It's very easy to miss one checkbox or answer a weirdly worded question wrong and end up getting an underpayment notice from the IRS.

If your only income is from a W-2 job and you take the standard deduction, DIY software can work well for you. But if your situation is more complicated, a tax professional can make sure everything is included and processed correctly.

If your tax return includes any of the following, consider working with a tax professional: small business, rental property, K-1s, investment income, cryptocurrency, foreign accounts, or multiple state tax returns. Another good reason: You've had a major change in your tax situation like getting married, having a child, or retiring. Life changes can change the tax picture in ways you may not expect. Some make you eligible or ineligible for certain tax credits; others affect your filing status. For the first filing year of a change, it can be helpful to have a tax professional navigate your new tax normal.

Also, if you dread doing your taxes or just don't want to deal with them, you can find a tax professional to take the job off your hands. Yes, you'll still have to pull the necessary information together, but then you can just sit back and relax while they do all the work.

HOW TO CHOOSE A TAX PREPARER

If you're going to pay someone to do your taxes, you want them done right. That means following the rules and minimizing your tax bill as much as possible. The second part, reducing your taxes as much as legally possible, calls for more than a single annual transaction, so consider looking for someone who offers tax planning services rather than just tax prep. After all, by the time you're filing taxes it's already too late to lower your tax bill.

Surprising to most people, you don't need any technical qualifications to be a paid tax preparer. The IRS does require that all paid preparers register with them and get a Preparer Tax Identification Number (PTIN), which takes about fifteen minutes and less than $20 to apply for.

Since tax laws can be confusing, tax planning calls for a thorough understanding of complex ideas. If you don't want to end up on the wrong side of an audit, it's in your best interest to work with a credentialed tax professional. Consider working with a certified public accountant (CPA), an enrolled agent (EA), or a tax attorney. While virtually anyone can prepare taxes, only credentialed professionals such as CPAs and EAs can represent you in front of the IRS. So in case of audit, you'll want to have one of those pros in your corner.

Before you hire anyone, make sure that they have the credentials you're looking for and that they'll e-file your tax return. You also want to verify that your paid preparer will sign your tax return, taking full responsibility for their work.

VITA AND TCE

Need help with your taxes but can't afford to hire a pro? The IRS offers free tax return assistance (primarily for basic returns) to qualified taxpayers. Volunteer Income Tax Assistance (VITA) is available for taxpayers including those who earn $64,000 or less, have disabilities, or speak limited English.

The Tax Counseling for the Elderly (TCE) program provides free tax prep for people at least sixty years old. This service specializes in senior tax issues, like retirement distributions and Social Security benefits.

While the IRS provides and administers these free tax services, they don't staff them. These tax preparers are all volunteers who must pass strict IRS vetting and training on issues that include taxpayer privacy and current tax law.

Verify Your Tax Preparer

The IRS provides a Directory of Federal Tax Return Preparers with Credentials and Select Qualifications for free online. This listing can help you find a tax preparer by location and qualification, and lets you verify a preparer's credentials in seconds. You can find the directory at https://irs.treasury.gov/rpo/rpo.jsf.

TAX PREPARER RED FLAGS

Tax returns contain a wealth of personal identifying and financial information, making them rich targets for scam artists posing as tax preparers. From your (and your family's) Social Security number to your annual income to your bank account numbers, you turn over your most sensitive documents to your tax professional, trusting that they'll keep them safe and private. Unfortunately, some tax preparers are criminals in business only to steal your information.

While it can be tricky to identify con artists, there are some glaring red flags to watch out for. For example, they don't have a PTIN, don't e-file and sign returns, or have no verifiable credentials. Even one of these red flags is reason enough to walk away. If you're not sure, look them up in the IRS Directory. If they're not listed, find someone else.

Chapter 7

Small Business Taxes

Even though most small businesses don't pay taxes on their own income, they still have to file tax returns. With the exception of C corporations, small business entities pass through their income (and losses) to the owners of the business. That income shows up on the business owners' tax returns as part of their personal taxable income.

These tax returns can be tricky to navigate, especially for first-time business owners. When they're not done correctly, that can result in IRS penalties, sometimes for both the business and the owner. Whether you hand this task off to a tax professional or decide to brave it and DIY, make sure all of your information—especially the business bookkeeping—is current and correct.

BUSINESS STRUCTURE DICTATES TAXATION

If You Build It, They Will Tax It

When you have your own business, the legal form of that business dictates the income tax forms you'll need to deal with. Every type of business structure has its own benefits and drawbacks, and that holds true for tax purposes as well. Some businesses pay their own taxes, while others pass their income through to the owner's personal tax returns (those are called pass-through entities).

SOLE PROPRIETORSHIPS

If you work for yourself and don't have any business partners, your business is a sole proprietorship by default unless you actively take steps to incorporate your business. Most freelancers, consultants, people with side gigs, self-employed people, and solo small business owners are sole proprietors. It's by far the most common business structure for small businesses. Any kind of business can operate as a sole proprietorship, and they can be part- or full-time gigs.

With this business form, there's no separation between the business and the business owner for legal or tax purposes. On the legal side, business liabilities are personal liabilities (and the other way around as well). On the tax side, the business income gets reported on your personal tax return on Schedule C. The income is also subject to self-employment taxes, reported on Schedule SE.

PARTNERSHIPS

When two or more people own an unincorporated business together, it's automatically considered a partnership. Every partner is automatically a general partner, 100% liable for all business debts and able to enter into contracts on behalf of the business.

Although you're not legally required to have a formal partnership agreement, it's smart to have one. Most small partnerships don't bother with this in the beginning but wish they had one when contentious issues arise. Partnership agreements spell out everything about the partnership. They normally include the designated tax matters partner (TMP), who represents the company on all matters related to taxes and the IRS. They'll also include each partner's roles and responsibilities in the company, each partner's ownership percentage, how profits (or losses) will be split for tax purposes, and when and how any distributions will be made.

Partnerships are pass-through entities, so they don't pay taxes on their income (at least for federal tax purposes). They are required to file informational federal and state tax returns; the federal return goes on Form 1065. All of the business income (or loss) passes through to the partners' personal income tax returns based on their partnership agreement or the default state rules if they don't have one. Each partner receives a Schedule K-1 detailing their share of income or losses, ownership (called capital), and other items relevant to their personal income tax returns.

C CORPORATIONS

C corporations, also known as regular corporations, are completely distinct tax entities. Each corporation counts as a "person," filing its own tax return and paying its own taxes. On the legal side, this separateness means that corporations, rather than shareholders or CEOs, deal with their own legal issues (sort of removing any personal responsibility from the picture). Owners of corporations are called stockholders or shareholders, and their percent ownership of the company depends on how many shares of stock they hold.

Corporations must be registered in the state they're formed, in the state where they maintain primary headquarters, and often in any states where they regularly do business. This can create the need to file multiple state tax returns and can often involve income, payroll, and sales tax liabilities along with any other relevant types of taxes. For income tax purposes, corporations must file Form 1120 annually.

Shareholders can generally be paid in two ways. If they work for the company, as is the case with many small corporations, they'll receive a regular paycheck. Shareholders, including shareholder-employees, may also receive dividends, which are a portion of the business profits. Corporate double taxation comes into play here: First the corporation pays taxes on its profits, and then the shareholders pay personal income tax on the portion of profits they receive as dividends. This can take a big bite of out income for very small or family-owned corporations.

S CORPORATIONS

S corporations work like C corporations for legal purposes but more like partnerships for tax purposes. S corporations are pass-through entities, so the business doesn't pay its own income taxes. Instead, the profits pass through to the personal tax returns of the shareholders based on their percent of ownership, which depends on the number of shares they hold.

Unlike with C corporations, there are many legal restrictions on S corporations. For example, they must be domestic (not foreign) corporations and they can't have more than one hundred share-holders. All individual shareholders must be US citizens or legal residents. Additionally, corporations and partnerships cannot own S corporation shares, but estates and certain types of trusts can own S corporation shares. Lastly, they can only have one class of stock.

To form an S corporation, the entity must complete and file IRS Form 2553, Election by a Small Business Corporation. When that's accepted by the IRS, the S corporation will be assigned its own federal tax ID number. Though S corporations don't pay tax on their profits, they must file annual information returns on IRS Form 1120-S.

Limited Liability Companies (LLCs)

LLCs are purely legal constructs designed to provide liability protection to small business owners. LLC owners are called members, and there's no limit on how many members there can be. LLCs get taxed based on their underlying business form. For example, a single-member LLC will be taxed as a sole proprietorship. A multi-member LLC will be taxed as a partnership. LLCs that actively elect to be taxed as corporations will file corporate tax returns. They can also choose to be taxed as either C or S corporations, as long as they meet the qualifications for S corporations and file Form 2553.

S corporation shareholders who work for the company (shareholder-employees) *must* be paid a regular and "reasonable" (according to the IRS) salary. Shareholders may receive distributions from the corporation, whether or not they work for the company. Shareholders will be taxed on their proportional share of profits (based on their ownership percentage) whether or not they receive distributions. Each shareholder will receive a Schedule K-1 at tax time detailing their share of the corporate profits and any other relevant tax items to use on their individual income tax returns.

WHAT COUNTS AS BUSINESS INCOME?

Everything Must Go (on Your Tax Return)

Business income can be confusing. While accountants and tax professionals mean "profit" when they say "income," many small business owners mean "revenue" when they use this term. In this section, we're talking about revenue, meaning money flowing into the business from its normal operations. That's what most people expect business income to include, but sometimes companies receive revenues in different ways, and those still count toward the total taxable profits.

More goes into business income than you might expect, and some of it may not be taxable on the federal level. This can include selling assets your business no longer needs, getting grants, or getting income on your business savings account. No matter what you've seen on social media, virtually all income your business earns will be taxable, so it's important to know what you have to report.

ORDINARY REVENUES

For a business, ordinary revenues include any money received in exchange for products or services, which can include (according to the IRS) professional service fees and rents received (for real estate businesses). Translation: All of your regular sales count as ordinary revenues. These sales are the main reason your business exists, and can include sales from different revenue streams. For example, a bookstore café would have two main sales pipelines: books and café items. But it could also sell things like bookmarks, knickknacks, and art supplies. Since all of those are still sold in the normal course of business, they're still ordinary revenues. Both in-person (like a local cupcake store) and online (like an Etsy shop) sales fit into this box. So, on your business tax form, this type of income would go in the box for "Gross receipts or sales," though it may be worded differently depending on the specific form.

AFFILIATE MARKETING

Affiliate marketing commissions often fit into the "other" income category for tax purposes. This revenue stream can generate passive income for an existing business, sometimes providing a substantial chunk of the company's cashflow. Affiliate marketing involves helping sell another company's products by referring customers there, often through a website link. Since the affiliate marketer isn't actually selling anything, there's no sales tax to deal with. But this does count as taxable income to the business.

Unfortunately, there's a lot of misinformation about affiliate sales and taxes out there. For example, there's no taxable income because you're not the one selling something, or you only have to pay tax if your affiliate income exceeds $600. Neither of those is true. Any income your business earns from any source is taxable, no matter the amount, and that absolutely includes income from affiliate marketing. Whether your company's affiliate marketing is unattached, related, or involved, any cash received from affiliate partners must be recorded on the books and included on the tax return.

BUSINESS GRANTS

Many small businesses receive grants every year, essentially gifts from granting agencies. They can be provided by federal, state, or local governments, large corporations, or nonprofit organizations, and the money does not have to be paid back in most cases.

Generally speaking, business grants count as income for federal tax purposes, though many states do not include these as taxable income (especially if they're state funded). If for some reason a business grant is tax-exempt, it will state that clearly in the grant agreement. For example, many grants offered throughout the COVID-19 crisis were tax-exempt for federal income tax purposes.

When your business receives grant money, the transaction needs to go on the books. The associated grant agreement will spell out how that money is to be spent and often includes a provision for dealing with the related income taxes.

"OTHER" INCOME

Even if it doesn't have anything to do with your revenues from your normal course of business, any money your company brings in can count as taxable income. If your business has an interest-bearing bank account or its own investment account (not a company retirement plan), any earnings on those accounts would be included in taxable income. Selling any property (other than inventory that you'd normally sell), such as an old van or a piece of equipment, also gets reported as business income but how it gets reported depends on the type of business. Royalties received for things like creating intellectual property (writing a book or composing music) also fall into this category.

COST OF GOODS SOLD

When you sell products, you've either had to create or purchase what you're selling. Either way, those products cost money. When people buy your products, the amount you paid for them transforms into "cost of goods sold" for tax and accounting purposes. Since the sale could not have existed if you didn't have the product available, cost of goods sold (or COGS) goes into the income portion of tax returns and financial statements rather than being included along with all of the other business expenses.

COGS includes any direct costs associated with purchasing or creating products for resale, such as the full cost of items bought for resale (including shipping fees), raw materials to make products, supplies used to produce products, labor to directly produce products, and packaging (like boxes that products will be sold or shipped in).

On the tax return, there's a special section for COGS calculations. The final COGS amount gets deducted from the gross sales to get to the company's gross profit.

What Doesn't Count As Income?

Not all money flowing into a business counts as income. Some of these non-taxable items include loan proceeds, capital contributions, early payment discounts from vendors, and insurance reimbursements (up to the amount of the loss to the business).

WHAT COUNTS AS A BUSINESS EXPENSE?

Can I Deduct This?

The IRS is very clear about what counts as a deductible business expense. To be deductible, an expense must be both ordinary and necessary. That said, business expenses basically include money you spend to help your business earn money on things expected to last for less than a year.

Business expenses help reduce taxable income, so not claiming all of your legitimate business expenses means you're paying too much in both income and self-employment (when applicable) taxes. That's why it's so important to carefully track all of your business expenditures and make sure nothing gets overlooked. Surprisingly, more people understate their business expenses than overstate them, but you want to make sure to not do either. The first step toward that is understanding what does and does not count as a business expense.

ASSETS VERSUS EXPENSES

Things that have long-term value to your business get treated differently than things you use up: think desks versus printer paper. Items like desks, trucks, and buildings are considered assets for accounting and tax purposes. Items like printer paper, insurance, wages, and web hosting are considered business expenses.

Because assets last a long time, their costs get spread out over their useful lives using accounting math called depreciation (more on that in a moment). Expenses, on the other hand, get deducted right away. So while you may have paid for a lot of things for your company, some of those things may not count as immediate business expenses for tax purposes. Though a company may not be able to write off the full cost of an asset when it's purchased, it can generally spread out that expense over time in the form of a depreciation or an amortization expense.

DEPRECIATION AND AMORTIZATION

Depreciation and amortization are special accounting expenses that serve to spread the cost of an asset over its useful life rather than deducting it all at once. This helps match up the cost of the asset with the period of time the business actually uses it. Depreciation is used for tangible (physical) assets like trucks, desks, and office buildings. Amortization is used for intangible assets like copyrights, patents, and trademarks.

The IRS provides depreciation methods and schedules for different types of assets. Straight-line depreciation is the most basic, dividing the total acquisition cost of the asset by its useful life. For example, your office furniture cost $7,000 and has a useful life of seven years, so annual depreciation expense would be $1,000 ($7,000 divided by seven years). Amortization also uses the straight-line method.

Other methods involve some form of accelerated expense, where the company gets a bigger tax deduction in the beginning that decreases over the life of the asset. The Modified Accelerated Cost Recovery System (MACRS) method is required by the IRS for all assets placed into service after 1986. The IRS provides guidance about which assets qualify for MACRS and what their useful lives should be (for tax purposes). The agency offers detailed tables for manually calculating MACRS depreciation, but it is built into most tax and accounting software.

Businesses also have the option to take advantage of bonus depreciation or Section 179 deduction for assets placed in service during the year. Bonus depreciation was greatly expanded under the TCJA and allows for a much larger first-year write off than MACRS. Originally, it allowed a 100% deduction in year one but that ended in 2022. For 2024 through 2027, the first-year bonus gradually decreases from 60% down to zero. Bonus depreciation is available for qualified assets with useful lives of twenty years or less and must have been purchased from an unrelated source (for example, you can't buy a delivery van from your cousin and use this method). Section 179 also allows for a bigger first-year depreciation expense. For 2024, you write off up to $1,220,000 assets purchased and put in service, but that amount begins to phase out if the total assets placed in service that year exceed $3,050,000. There's a limited Section 179 deduction of $30,500 for SUVs for 2024. You can find out more about the qualifications and assets eligible for bonus deprecation or Section 179 on the IRS website at www.irs.gov.

WHAT'S NOT A BUSINESS EXPENSE?

While social media may have you believing that almost everything counts as a business expense, that's just not true. To qualify as a business expense, it must be ordinary and necessary. Here, "ordinary expense" means that other businesses in your industry would commonly have this same expense. For example, in a veterinarian's office, dog treats would count as an ordinary business expense. "Necessary expense," according to the IRS, means an expenditure that is "helpful and appropriate," but it doesn't have to be indispensable. For example, expenses like employee wages and utilities may be necessary to run your business.

There's a lot of bad advice and misinformation out there about claiming business expenses, especially when they cross the line into personal expenses. Some common myths include paying with business cash or credit cards automatically makes something a business expense; eating lunch at your desk counts as a business lunch; buying a special outfit for a client meeting is a normal business expense; or, if you post about it, any personal expense can be treated as a business expense. The IRS is clear that these are simply untrue!

PAYING YOURSELF

Paying yourself counts as a tax-deductible business expense sometimes in some business structures, but not in others. If you're a corporate shareholder-employee on payroll, your regular paycheck and all of the associated taxes would be fully deductible by the business. If you're a partner receiving guaranteed payments, those payments are deductible by the partnership.

Other than that, paying yourself generally would not constitute a business tax deduction. Sole proprietors cannot be on payroll, and when they take money out of the business for personal reasons, it's never deductible. Non-salary payments to shareholders aren't deductible either and count as distributions to S corporation owners or dividends to C corporation owners. When partners receive money or assets beyond their guaranteed compensation, those payments are considered distributions.

Guaranteed Payments to Partners

Guaranteed payments serve as compensation for partners in a partnership, similar to salary but without any taxes withheld by the company. Partners receive these regular payments regardless of business profits. These guaranteed payments are deductible to the partnership and count as taxable income to the partner, also subject to self-employment taxes.

HOME OFFICE EXPENSE DEDUCTION

If you're self-employed and use part of your home for work, you may be able to use the home office deduction. The rules are strict, but if you qualify, it makes sense to take this valuable deduction to reduce both your income and self-employment taxes.

First, the rules. In order to take the home office deduction, the space must be used *exclusively and regularly* for your business. "Exclusively" here means that you absolutely do not use that space for anything else. So if you're working off your kitchen table, your bed, or your couch, those wouldn't pass the exclusive use test. If you converted a closet into a workspace and use it only for that, then the closet would count as a home office. For this rule, "regularly" means you use this space as your main place of business. If you have an outside business space, like a salon chair or a shop, your home office may still qualify if you use it regularly for things like billing, bookkeeping, or other management duties.

Once you've passed the exclusive and regular tests, you have two options for calculating your home office deduction. In the simplified method, you multiply the square footage of your workspace (up to 300 square feet maximum) by the IRS rate, currently $5 per square foot. The regular method prorates whole-home expenses based on the proportion of your office space. For example, if your office is 100 square feet and your whole home is 1,000 square feet, you could deduct 10% (100/1000) of expenses such as rent, mortgage interest, utilities, security, cleaning, property taxes, home insurance, and depreciation.

Under the regular method, you can also deduct 100% of direct expenses, meaning expenses that are just for the office space. For example, if you have a cleaning service just for the office and not for the whole home, you could deduct that full expense.

Many taxpayers are afraid to deduct legitimate home office expenses for fear it will increase their risk of being audited—that it's a red flag to the IRS. This is not true. But if you're worried, make sure to document your use of the office space and all of the related expenses. Take pictures that clearly demonstrate its use as a workplace. Avoid using the space for anything else. A legitimate expense serves as a reasonable defense in the case of an audit, so plan to show up with receipts.

SCHEDULE C: SOLE PROPRIETORSHIPS

Wait, I'm a Business?

If you own your business by yourself and have not formed a corporation, your business is considered a sole proprietorship for tax purposes. That's true even if you have formed a single-member LLC because those don't exist in the tax world (they're legal structures only). According to the Small Business Administration, 86.5% of small businesses without employees—more than 19 million companies—fall into this category.

Some sole proprietors don't realize they're business owners at first. You don't actually have to have a full-on business. Any 1099-NEC income, which reports non-employee compensation (independent contractor pay) you earn puts you squarely into this category. So whether you have a side gig, work as a freelancer or consultant, or own a bookstore, you are a business owner and a sole proprietor. That means you have to pay the extra 15.3% in self-employment taxes, but it also means you can deduct business expenses from your earnings—something W-2 employees can't do.

Sole proprietorships don't file their own tax returns. Rather, their income (or loss) gets filed as part of the owner's personal income tax return with the business information reported on Schedule C.

WHAT GOES ON SCHEDULE C?

Schedule C includes all sorts of information about your business, along with its revenues and expenses. The first section asks for the company name, address, and tax identification number if any are different than yours. It also asks for the principal business or profession, which is your company's primary source of revenues, along with the principal business or professional activity code.

The second section asks questions about some tax-related general business information. In this part you'll include your accounting method (which is "cash basis" for most small businesses), whether you "materially participated" in the business (which will be "yes" for most small business owners), whether the business was started in the current tax year (checked for the first year in business only), whether the business made payments that would require it to file Forms 1099 (for any contractor paid $600 or more during the year), and if required 1099s were or will be sent.

Principal Business or Professional Activity Code

Business activity codes are six-digit numbers from the North American Industry Classification System (NAICS) that help the IRS track statistical information. They also give the IRS an edge when looking at business returns, including Schedule C, to make sure the revenues and expenses make sense. From the more than 1,000 codes, choose the one that's the best match for your main business.

The next section gets down to the numbers, the revenues, costs, and expenses for the year, separated into Parts I through V. For businesses that use any form of bookkeeping software, all of this information can be found on the Profit and Loss Statement. The Schedule C follows the same basic format. It starts with revenues (or sales) and other forms of business income (like interest income or grants) followed by a cost of goods sold section for companies that sell products, and finally a listing of business expenses. There's a special section for business use of a personal vehicle on page two of this Schedule, and those total expenses flow back to page one. After the total expenses, there's a line showing the profit or loss before calculating any home office expenses. That's followed by the home office expense information, and then the final net profit or loss. That bottom-line number gets carried to Schedule 1 and also to Schedule SE (to figure your self-employment taxes).

SELF-EMPLOYMENT TAXES

When you have your own business, you'll need to deal with self-employment taxes (Social Security and Medicare), where you basically have to pay both sides of the employment tax (employer and employee). The exception: If you have less than $400 of self-employment earnings, you generally won't have to deal with it.

Self-employment tax gets calculated on 92.35% of your Schedule C income (this subtracts the 7.65%, half of self-employment tax that would normally be paid by the employee). That gets multiplied by 15.3%, which includes 12.4% for Social Security and 2.9% for Medicare. This tax gets calculated on Schedule SE, which gets included with your Form 1040. Here's how the calculation works:

Suppose you had $50,000 of net income on your Schedule C. You would owe self-employment taxes on $46,175 of that ($50,000 × 0.9235). The self-employment tax would come out to $7,064.78 ($46,175 × 0.153). That amount would be added to your total taxes due.

Unlike income tax, there are no deductions from self-employment tax. Even if you don't owe any income taxes, you can still owe self-employment taxes. This often comes as a surprise to taxpayers, especially if they haven't been making estimated tax payments throughout the year.

SELF-EMPLOYED HEALTH INSURANCE DEDUCTION

If you're self-employed and pay for your own health insurance, you can get a special above-the-line federal income tax deduction for that. If you qualify, you can deduct all premiums paid for medical (including dental, vision, and long-term care) insurance for you, your spouse, your dependents, and your non-dependent children up to age twenty-six.

This deduction is separate from your business deductions and doesn't go on your Schedule C. Instead, it's a special personal tax deduction that goes on Schedule 1 as an "adjustment to income."

To qualify for this deduction, you can't have any other health coverage. That means if you have a business and a W-2 job that offers you a health plan, you can't take the deduction. You also can't take it if your spouse could participate in an employer-based health plan. The deduction is also limited by your business income. If your business breaks even or has a loss for the year, this deduction won't be available.

FORM 1065: PARTNERSHIPS

We'll File These Taxes Together

When two or more people own a business together and have not formed a corporation, they have a partnership. Partnerships have to file informational tax returns on IRS Form 1065. These tax returns can be extensive depending on the type of business, the number of partners, and any special issues that the business deals with. The point of the 1065 is to furnish the federal government with information about the business, its accounting method (cash or accrual), its current year profits (or losses), the partners, and their share of the profits that will be reported on their personal tax returns. Because the partners will need this information to prepare their own tax returns, partnership returns are due on March 15, one month before the individual income tax filing due date.

Spouse Partnerships

Two spouses who own a business together as a partnership or multi-member LLC generally have to file Form 1065 for the business. The exception: a qualified joint venture, which allows them to report their respective shares of company income on separate Schedule Cs. There are lots of rules to follow here, so check with a tax professional before filing the business tax return.

These tax returns are extensive and complicated, and it's best to work with a professional tax preparer rather than try to DIY. Errors on the Form 1065 flow out to all of the partners' individual income tax returns, potentially causing tax issues for all parties involved.

FORM 1065

The main income tax form partnerships (including multi-member LLCs that have not incorporated) complete is IRS Form 1065. Like most tax forms, it starts with general information about the business such as the main business activity, the main product or service provided, the company's EIN (federal tax ID number), their original start date, and their business code number.

The rest of the first page is devoted to income (revenue) and expenses, leading to the overall net business's profit or loss. There is a small additional section on this first page that most small businesses probably won't need to deal with; it involves circumstances where the partnership itself may owe some taxes.

Pages two and three, also called Schedule B, focuses on other information. There's a list of thirty questions, some with sub-questions, with yes/no answers. For many small business partnerships, most of these won't apply. A few probably will, such as whether the business had any debt forgiven during the year or whether 1099s were provided to all applicable contractors.

Page four, known as Schedule K, is another important piece of the 1065. Schedule K covers "Partners' Distributive Share Items," meaning all of the individual tax items that will be allocated to the partners. This includes things like the profit or loss for the year, charitable contributions made, earnings subject to self-employment, nondeductible expenses, and tax-exempt income. Only items appearing on Schedule K will make their way onto the partners' Schedule K-1.

Finally, the last page includes Schedule L (Balance Sheets per Books), Schedule M-1 [Reconciliation of Income (Loss) per Books With Analysis of Net Income (Loss) per Return], and Schedule M-2 (Analysis of Partners' Capital Accounts). Schedule L is a copy of the company's balance sheet for the appropriate tax year, part of their regular financial statements. Schedule M-1 accounts for any differences between book and tax income, which could include things like tax-exempt income and nondeductible expenses. Schedule M-2 tracks the total ownership of the business for the year, from the beginning capital balances to their year-end balances. This takes into account things like annual income (or loss), any capital added to the company by a partner (or partners), and distributions to the partners.

PARTNER ALLOCATIONS AND DISTRIBUTIONS

Each partner has their own piece of the company, usually based on the partnership agreement and the amount of capital they contributed to the partnership. Their shares of income, gains, losses, credits, and deductions are called allocations, basically how everything gets divvied up. Each partner's share of these tax items passes through to their personal tax returns, as reported on their Schedule K-1. General partners pay both income and self-employment taxes on their share of company profits.

Special allocations occur when an item gets divided up in a different way rather than based on ownership percentages. For example, two partners may own a business equally with one partner doing more of the day-to-day work, and that can be reflected in a special allocation where that partner receives 60% of the profits.

Partners take money and property from the business as distributions (for tax purposes). Distributions that resemble salaries are called "guaranteed payments to partners," where each partner gets paid a set amount regardless of profits at that time. Guaranteed payments are deductible expenses for the partnership. Individual partners pay both income and self-employment taxes on their guaranteed payments for the year.

All other transfers from the partnership to the partners are regular distributions. Generally, distributions themselves aren't subject to additional taxes. However, if partners take distributions that exceed their stake in the business (which can happen when the company borrows money), those may trigger additional taxes.

SCHEDULE K-1

When the Form 1065 is completed, a Schedule K-1 will be generated for each partner to use on their individual tax returns. These schedules contain a wealth of tax-related information and generally include instructions on where each amount goes on the partner's tax return.

Schedule K-1 has three sections:

1. Part I contains information about the partnership such as its name, main address, and tax ID number.
2. Part II contains information about the partner including their tax ID, name, and contact details along with partnership-related items. These include whether they're a general or limited partner; their share of profits, losses, and capital; their share of liabilities; and their capital account analysis. This analysis is a summary of how their ownership stake changed during the year due to capital contributions, distributions, the current year's profit (or loss), and more.

3. Part III details the "Partner's Share of Current Year Income, Deductions, Credits, and Other Items," breaking down each into smaller pieces. For example, the K-1 includes separate lines for things like business income (loss), rental income (loss), guaranteed payments, interest income, other income (loss), Section 179 deduction, self-employment earnings, credits, tax-exempt income and nondeductible expenses, and distributions.

Schedule K-1 can be tricky to navigate, even with professional tax software, so it's important to verify that all of the information is correct. If it's wrong for one partner, it may be wrong for all of them, especially if the problem involves partner allocations.

FORM 1120: CORPORATIONS

Making Money, Paying Taxes

Corporations, also called C corporations or regular corporations, are the only business entities that pay their own federal income taxes. They use Form 1120 to report their income and taxes due, with a regular filing deadline of April 15. The form has to be filed every year whether or not the company has any taxable income. Like all business income tax forms, there's a portion of the return that resembles standard financial statements. However, Form 1120 also contains an extensive question list that must be answered on its Schedule K.

FORM 1120

The first section of Form 1120 asks for details about the corporation. These include the name of the corporation, its incorporation date, its tax ID number, its mailing address, and its total assets as of the last day of the tax year.

The income section of the return is next. It starts with regular sales and cost of goods sold to get to the gross profit, then goes into other types of income. Some of the additional forms of income require extra forms. For example, when corporations earn dividends (from other corporations), they have to complete a special schedule. The income section is followed by deductions, including regular business expenses, to get to the net income.

If a corporation doesn't earn any income from investments in other corporations (and most small business corporations don't), the next section—Schedule C—can be skipped. The next section is for all corporations: Schedule J, Tax Computation and Payment. This is where the tax on corporate income gets calculated, payments made during the year get reported, and business credits can be taken. Currently, the federal corporate income tax rate is 21%; state corporate income rates vary.

General Business Credit

Many small businesses qualify for the General Business Credit, a collection of tax credits that promote small businesses. These get reported in summary on Form 3800, which can include dozens of credits, after being reported on individual tax credit forms. These include the Small Business Health Care Tax Credit, the Work Opportunity Tax Credit, and the Employer Credit for Paid Family and Medical Leave.

SCHEDULES K, L, M-1, AND M-2

All corporations must complete Schedule K, Other Information as part of their annual federal income tax return. Along with general information such as the business activity code and the corporation's accounting method, there are two pages of detailed questions to answer. Most small business corporations will answer "no" to most of the questions, but some will commonly be answered "yes." For example, Line 4b asks whether anyone owned more than 20% of the company, which is the case for most small corporations. Line 13 asks if the corporation had both less than $250,000 in gross receipts and $250,000 in assets at the end of the year; most small corporations can answer "yes" to this, removing the requirement to complete Schedules L, M-1, and M-2.

Though corporations that answer "yes" to Line 13 don't have to complete Schedule L, Balance Sheets per Books, many do anyway to help keep track for future years. This form includes exactly what it sounds like, the corporation's balance sheet at the end of the year.

Schedule M-1 is used to reconcile any differences between the books and the tax returns. These are common due to things like non-deductible expenses and nontaxable income. Schedule M-2 is used to analyze the changes in retained earnings during the year.

SHAREHOLDERS AND EMPLOYEES

Small corporations are often also closely held, meaning they have five or fewer shareholders that own more than half of the total shares. It's very common for at least one of these shareholders to also work for the business as an employee. Shareholder-employees get regular salary through payroll, which is a deductible expense for the corporation.

To avoid double taxation, many shareholder-employees try to make their salaries as high as possible. However, the IRS has a reasonable compensation rule that can cause headaches. There's no set IRS formula to calculate an appropriate salary, so it's really up to the discretion of the shareholders. Some accountants recommend a sixty-forty split, where 60% of distributions to the shareholder are considered as salary and 40% as dividends, but that's just a guideline. As long as there's reasonable justification for the salary (like it's industry standard) and at least some of the income is distributed as dividends (when there's enough income to distribute), the IRS may leave it alone.

DIVIDENDS AND 1099S

Small corporations, especially those with only one shareholder, try to avoid the double taxation associated with paying dividends. They might try to do this by paying themselves as much salary as possible, avoiding the need to take any other kind of distributions. The IRS looks at this area and may reclassify what they consider excess salary as dividends.

When corporations do pay dividends to their shareholders, they must prepare and send Form 1099-DIV—even if there's only one shareholder. This includes all non-salary distributions to owners of the corporation regardless of their ownership percentage. These forms must be sent out by March 31 each year.

Many small business corporation owners mistakenly think they don't need to send these 1099-DIVs to themselves, but they do. The IRS charges non-filing penalties starting at $50 per form.

Double Taxation

Double taxation means that the same income gets taxed twice. This happens with corporations where income is first taxed to the company and then taxed again when it's distributed to shareholders as dividends.

FORM 1120-S: S CORPORATIONS

Just Passing Through

Like C corporations, S corporations file their own tax returns, but that's where the similarities end. S corporations are considered pass-through entities. The company itself doesn't pay any federal taxes, but instead passes its income through to its shareholders' personal tax returns. These tax returns take a detailed look at all aspects of the company, from its individual shareholders to its financial picture.

REASONABLE SALARY

One of the key tax benefits of S corporations is the ability to minimize self-employment taxes while still pulling money out of the business. Shareholder-employees have two types of income to deal with: their salary and their share of profits. The salary is subject to both income and payroll taxes, but the profits are only subject to income taxes. So to minimize the total tax bite, they have an incentive to keep the salary as low as possible.

Enter the "reasonable compensation" rule. The IRS requires S corporation shareholder-employees to take a reasonable salary for their position. This can be a gray area, and one with some wiggle room. But you'll want to make sure you can make a good case for reasonable salary to avoid any reclassification issues with the IRS. If an auditor deems the salary to not be reasonable, they can recharacterize more of your income as salary. That can lead to a bill for back taxes and stiff tax penalties.

So, what counts as reasonable? It depends on the income produced for the corporation by the shareholder. For example, if all of the corporate income is based on services provided by the shareholder (like coaching or consulting work), a bigger share of the income would be considered salary than if non-shareholder employees did most of the income-producing work and the shareholder merely managed them. A good rule of thumb: Use the salary that the shareholder would earn if they worked for a different company, a reasonable salary for the position.

ACCOUNTABLE PLANS

Sometimes as a shareholder-employee you'll use personal money to pay for business expenses. For example, you might have put business travel expenses on your personal credit card. Or you might have mixed expenses, which include things you use for both business and personal purposes like your phone or Internet.

In order for the S corporation to be able to deduct those expenses you paid with personal funds, the business has to reimburse you for them. That's where the accountable plan comes in to play. Accountable plans allow employers (the S corporation in this case) to reimburse employees (you) for out-of-pocket business expenses without any tax consequences for the employee. If the business doesn't have an accountable plan, things could get sticky tax-wise.

For expenses to be allowable under an accountable plan, they must be business-related and reported accurately and timely. In addition, any excess reimbursements have to be returned to the company. Without an accountable plan, reimbursements paid to employees can be reclassified as compensation by the IRS and would be subject to taxes.

Since S corporation shareholder-employees often pay for business expenses (especially mixed expenses) with personal funds, it makes sense to set up an accountable plan. All it takes is a simple document stating the terms of the plan (for example, how often employees need to submit expense reports) to create one. You can ask your tax professional to help you create the accountable plan document to avoid any potential issues down the line.

Home Office Expenses

An accountable plan can also cover home office expenses if you use that space regularly and exclusively for the business. Figure out the business percentage of your home based on square footage and apply that percentage to expenses like rent, mortgage interest, property taxes, and utilities. Document these expenses and the accountable plan can reimburse you for them periodically.

FORM 1120-S

S corporations don't pay their own taxes, but they do have to file informational tax returns every year using IRS Form 1120-S. Like other business tax returns, this form starts with information about the company including its name and mailing address, the S election effective date (the first date the corporation intended to be treated as an S corporation), business activity code, tax identification number, incorporation date, total assets on the last day of the tax year, and number of shareholders.

The next section follows the basic format of a Profit and Loss Statement. It starts with total revenues from regular business activities and cost of goods sold to calculate the gross profit. Any other income (like business grants or interest) gets listed right after that to get to the total income (or loss). Next are the corporation's regular business expenses, which get subtracted from total income to come up with the ordinary business income (or loss).

The final section on page one addresses taxes and tax payments. This section applies to S corporations that formerly operated as C corporations.

Next, Schedule B requires more detailed information about the corporation and its owners. That's followed by Schedule K, Shareholders' Pro Rata Share Items, which contains summary information of what will flow to the individual shareholders' Schedules K-1.

S corporations with both total receipts for the year of less than $250,000 and total assets at the end of the year totaling less than $250,000 don't have to complete Schedules L (the Balance Sheets per Books) and M-1 (the reconciliation between the books and the tax return). Finally, all S corporations must complete Schedule M-2, Analysis of Accumulated Adjustments Account, Shareholders' Undistributed Taxable Income Previously Taxed, Accumulated Earnings and Profits, and Other Adjustments Account. This schedule basically reconciles all of the accounts that affect shareholders' basis, the value of their total capital investment in the company.

SCHEDULE K-1

When the Form 1120-S is completed, a Schedule K-1 will be generated for each shareholder to use on their individual tax return. These schedules contain a wealth of tax-related information and generally include instructions on where each amount goes on the shareholder's tax return.

Schedule K-1 has three sections:

1. Part I contains information about the S corporation such as its name, main address, tax ID number, and total number of shares.
2. Part II contains information about the shareholder including their tax ID, name, and contact details. It also includes their current year allocation percentage, their number of shares at the beginning and end of the tax year, and the total amount of loans from the shareholder to the corporation at the beginning and end of the tax year.
3. Part III details the "Shareholder's Share of Current Year Income, Deductions, Credits, and Other Items," breaking down each into smaller pieces. For example, the K-1 includes separate lines for ordinary business income (loss), net rental real estate income (loss), interest income, Section 179 deduction, credits, alternative minimum tax (AMT) items, items affecting shareholder basis, and other information.

Schedule K-1 reports the income, deduction, credit, and other tax items applicable to the shareholder. In small S corporations, where the owners are also employees, those shareholders will also receive Forms W-2 (for their salaries) and Forms 1099-DIV (for any other distributions they took from the company).

Chapter 8

Dealing With the IRS

Getting a letter from the IRS ranks up in the top fears of many Americans; it's as scary as snakes, spiders, and killer clowns. However, the truth is that most interaction with the IRS isn't as bad as you'd think. Most of the time, there are simple solutions. Sometimes, they'll even want to give you money back.

The most important thing you can do when the IRS contacts you is to respond. Ignoring the communication will only make things worse. Without input from you, the IRS wins by default, and they're not always right. So if you get a letter from the IRS, open it and read it. In some cases, you'll be able to deal with it yourself, often through your online account. If you need help, get in contact with your tax professional (or find one) or contact the IRS Taxpayer Advocate Service.

CREATING YOUR ONLINE ACCOUNT

Set Me Up

One of the easiest ways to stay on top of your personal tax situation is to create your online IRS account. You'll have access to a lot of your tax-related information such as tax transcripts, IRS notices, and payments made. You'll also be able to make payments, set up payment plans, and electronically sign Power of Attorney authorizations for your tax professional. Overall, it's the simplest way to look up details about your federal taxes and can make your life a lot easier when dealing with the IRS.

HOW TO CREATE YOUR IRS ACCOUNT

To get this whole process started, go to the IRS website home page at www.irs.gov and select "Sign in to your account." This will bring you to the "Your account" page, where you can create an account by clicking on the "Sign in to online account" button. From there, you'll have the option to create your account by clicking on the button that says "ID.me Create an account." Enter your email address, create a secure password, and click on the "Create account" button. That will send you over to the ID.me site for identity verification.

To set up your online IRS account, you'll need to go through an identity verification process by creating an ID.me account. That requires an official photo ID, like a passport or driver's license, and a live selfie on the website. Once your identification has been verified, you'll be able to log in to your IRS online account. You then can set up your profile and begin accessing the needed information about your federal taxes.

WHAT YOU'LL FIND ONLINE

Once you have your account set up, you'll find a ton of information and tools you can use. When you log in, you'll be sent to your own IRS home page, which serves as a general overview. It includes things like whether they've processed your current year's tax return, notification preferences, payment information, and a way to view your tax records, including correspondence from the IRS.

From this page, you can easily navigate to what you want to do. For example, you can choose to go paperless and receive certain IRS notices online rather than through the mail. You can find your current account balance, look at summary information for the prior year's tax return, or get copies of your tax transcripts, which include salary and interest income reported by third parties with your Social Security number.

Another feature: You can view, accept, or reject requests for Power of Attorney (POA) or Tax Information Authorization (TIA). These are typically requested by tax professionals you've hired to help you with a tax issue. POAs give your professional the authority to represent you in tax matters before the IRS and to look at your tax information for any tax matters and tax years that you allow. TIAs allow a person (or corporation or other organization) the ability to view or receive your confidential tax information but not to act on your behalf.

You can also complete Form 4506-T, Request for Transcript of Tax Return, that allows someone to view specific tax information for things like income verification when you apply for a loan.

USE IT TO MANAGE PAYMENTS

One of the most often used features of the IRS online account is payment management. In this section of your account, you can look at all of your payment activity. There's a screen to view scheduled and pending payments so you know what's coming up. It also offers a full listing of all of your payments that the IRS has already processed, which can come in handy if you don't remember how much you paid for your first quarter estimate, for example.

Payment management also gives you the opportunity to make payments and set up online payment plans if you can't pay your balance in full. When you go to make a payment, make sure to choose the right reason for your payment so the IRS applies it correctly. For example, your payment options may include pay 20XX income tax (where "XX" stands for the prior tax year, like tax year 2024 in filing year 2025), pay toward your balance due, amended return (if you made changes to your tax return and it changed how much you owed), or estimated tax (for the current tax year).

You can choose the amount, payment date, and bank account you want the payment pulled from. This allows you to schedule estimated tax payments ahead of time, for example, to make sure you never miss a due date.

MANAGE PAYMENT PLANS

Through your online account, you can apply for a payment plan if you have a balance due. (If you recently filed your tax return and it's not showing the balance yet, you may not be able to apply this way until your account is updated.) It generally takes less than twenty minutes to apply. Once you've completed the application process, you'll be notified immediately if it's been accepted.

If you have an existing payment plan (or plans) with the IRS, you'll see the details of that on the home page of your online account that includes the type of plan, the payment amount, and the payment due date. From there, you can update your payment agreement if necessary, including reinstating a plan after missing enough payments to default.

Dealing With Notices

As of May 2024, the IRS allows for nine types of notices to be resolved by taxpayers online and plans to expand the functionality to additional notices in the future. Currently, through the IRS Document Upload Tool, taxpayers can respond to issues surrounding the Child Tax Credit, Premium Tax Credit, and Earned Income Tax Credit. You can use the tool whether or not you have an online account, but you'll find any applicable notices there.

FILING AND PAYING TAXES ONLINE

Click and Pay

Filing taxes and making payments online is your best option for speed, security, and convenience. No standing in line at the post office. No having to find your checkbook and your payment voucher. No worries about lost or delayed mail. The IRS offers many options for both filing your taxes online for free and making payments. The site is easy to navigate and use; it also uses high-end encryption to protect your information.

IRS DIRECT FILE

In tax season 2024 (for filing 2023 tax returns), the IRS launched a pilot program called IRS Direct File. It allows certain taxpayers in twelve test states to file their income tax returns online directly with the IRS for free. The twelve states include Arizona, California, Florida, Massachusetts, Nevada, New Hampshire, New York, South Dakota, Tennessee, Texas, Washington, and Wyoming. To qualify to use this program, taxpayers can only have certain types of income including W-2 wages, Social Security, unemployment compensation, and $1,500 or less of interest income. Additionally, they can claim only three tax credits including the Earned Income Tax Credit, Child Tax Credit, and the Credit for Other Dependents. Finally, they have to take the standard deduction and must limit above-the-line deductions to student loan interest and educator expenses.

Along with the ability to file directly with the IRS for free, this program offers a step-by-step guide to help taxpayers understand their returns and live online support from IRS staff. The program doesn't currently support state income tax filing, though some states allow information to transfer directly from IRS Direct File to their online tax tools. Unfortunately, the program does not pre-populate taxpayers' information, so it needs to be typed in like with any other tax software.

The IRS plans to expand this program to all fifty states and include more functionality for taxpayers who may have different kinds of income or claim additional credits and deductions.

Direct File Results Are In

For its inaugural tax season, the IRS Direct File pilot program was used to process more than 140,000 tax returns, collected $35 million in taxes owed, and sent out more than $90 million in refunds. According to the IRS, more than 90% of filers ranked their experiences as "above average" or "excellent," citing the ease of use and trustworthiness.

IRS FREE E-FILE OPTIONS

A lot of software companies claim to offer "free" income tax filing, but when taxpayers go to file, it turns out there are fees. To use true free file tax programs, you'll want to go directly through the IRS website and not through any individual software company. That's not to say all free file offerings are scams—they're not—but there have been thousands of incidents where people thought they were getting completely free tax filing and they weren't. Bottom line: Start your free file through the IRS website at https://apps.irs.gov/app/freefile. When you do that, free means free. According to the IRS, "As long as you meet the eligibility criteria for the IRS Free File trusted partner's offer you selected, you must not be charged for the electronic preparation and filing of a federal tax return."

The IRS offers this free guided tax software for taxpayers with AGI of $79,000 or less (for 2024, AGI maximum may change). The partner programs may have additional qualifications before you can use them. Some (but not all) also offer free state filing. You can choose to look at all the available partner programs or choose a specific one using a directed IRS tool. There's a filter to help you narrow down the options based on a few criteria like whether you're active military or will be claiming the Earned Income Tax Credit, for example.

As of 2024, eight companies are IRS trusted partners; they include TaxSlayer, TaxAct, and FreeTaxUSA. Remember to go through the IRS site to make sure you access the truly free version.

FREE FILLABLE FORMS

If you make too much money or otherwise don't qualify for IRS Free File, you can still file your taxes for free using the online fillable forms on the IRS website. This takes more know-how than the guided tax software most people are used to. You'll need to know which forms you need and which spaces need to be filled, and the software will do the math. Some values, such as AGI, may transfer automatically between forms, but most don't. It's basically the same as doing your tax return with pen and paper, but you can e-file it.

To create your account for this filing option, you'll need to have a US phone number that can accept text messages. You'll also need to create a new account every year. The Free Fillable Forms program does allow you to e-file your return with the IRS but does not have any state income tax return capabilities. This filing option closes mid-October every year, right after the extended tax return due date, and your return will not be accessible to view, print, or file after that.

HOW TO MAKE PAYMENTS

If you don't have an IRS online account (or even if you do, actually) you can make tax payments directly on the IRS website. Whether you have a balance due on your tax return, need to pay quarterly estimates, want to make a payment on an installment plan, or owe the IRS money for some other reason, you can submit your payment through their website.

The best option is Direct Pay, which will directly debit a savings or checking account for whatever amount you specify. There are no extra fees for paying this way. As soon as you make the payment, you'll get a confirmation number for your records. You can make up to two Direct Pay payments in a twenty-four-hour period (like if you wanted to pay your tax bill and make an estimated tax payment). If you need to make more than two payments, you'll have to wait until the next day to make the third.

Other payment options on the website include using a debit or credit card or paying through digital wallets like PayPal or Venmo. These options all come with processing fees (they go to the payment processors, not to the IRS) that run from a minimum $2.20 for debit card payments and 1.82% for credit card and digital wallet payments.

No matter which payment method you choose, make sure that you choose the right tax year and tax type when submitting your payment. You can choose the amount and the payment date that work best for you.

IF YOU CAN'T PAY YOUR WHOLE TAX BILL

Try the Layaway Plan

Every year, millions of Americans face tax bills that they can't pay all at once. The IRS has several ways to help you manage your tax debt, and most of them are better for your finances than paying your taxes by credit card. There are short- and long-term payment plans, special hardship extensions for payments, and offers in compromise to settle an overwhelming tax debt. Figuring out which option to use depends on your situation, including how much you owe and how long it would realistically take you to pay it off. As soon as you apply for a payment plan, the IRS generally can't place any levies on your assets and their time to collect gets suspended, giving you some breathing room. The most important thing here is to pay as much as you can by the due date and take proactive steps to deal with your tax balance. Controlling your options is better than having the IRS come after you.

SHORT-TERM PAYMENT PLANS

If you owe the IRS $100,000 or less (total combined taxes, interest, and penalties) and can pay off your entire balance within 180 days, you can apply for a short-term payment plan online. You do this by logging into (or creating) your IRS online account and completing an Online Payment Agreement (OPA) application. There are no application or setup fees for these plans, but penalties and interest will keep piling up until the debt is paid in full.

You'll have three main options for making the payments: Direct Pay, where you set up direct debit payments from your savings or checking account; electronic payments through the Electronic Federal Tax Payment System (EFTPS), which you can enroll in on their website at www.eftps.gov; or monthly payments by check, credit card, debit card, or money order.

If your situation changes, you can revise your payment plan online. Using the Online Payment Agreement tool, you'll be able to change the payment amount, the monthly due date, and the bank information for Direct Pay (if you want to switch bank accounts). You can also switch your existing payment method to Direct Pay with the tool.

If for some reason you can't apply online, you can complete IRS Form 9465, Installment Agreement Request, and mail it in. You can also apply by phone by calling 1-800-829-1040.

LONG-TERM PAYMENT PLANS

If you owe the IRS $50,000 or less (including taxes, interest, and penalties), you can qualify for a long-term payment plan, also called an installment agreement. This gives you a longer time to pay your tax bill, up to six years of monthly payments. Until the full balance is paid off, the IRS will continue to add on interest and penalties.

If you set up automatic debit withdrawals through a Direct Debit installment agreement, you'll pay a $31 fee to apply online or a $107 fee to apply by phone, by mail, or in person. Low-income taxpayers may be able to get these setup fees waived. Taxpayers who owe more than $25,000 have to use this payment method.

If you choose to pay another way, the setup fees are higher. This includes all payments that are not automatic direct debit withdrawals such as Direct Pay (where it's a direct debit but you have to initiate it), check, money order, or credit card. It costs $130 to apply online or $225 to apply via phone, mail, or in person. Low-income taxpayers get charged a $43 fee but may be able to get that fee reimbursed later. Additional fees will also apply when you pay by card.

HARDSHIP EXTENSION TO PAY

The IRS offers the option for taxpayers to apply for hardship extensions but rarely grants them. Still, if you qualify, you can submit IRS Form 1127, Application for Extension of Time for Payment of Tax Due to Undue Hardship, to request six months extra time to pay the taxes you owe. Along with your identifying information and the amount and type of tax you owe, you'll have to provide a detailed explanation of your undue hardship. According to the IRS, this means that you will "sustain a substantial financial loss if required to pay a tax or deficiency on the due date." You'll also have to include supporting documentation such as a statement of your net worth (everything you own and everything you owe) along with an itemized budget of all of your income and expenses for the three-month period prior to the tax due date.

Offer in Compromise

An offer in compromise gives taxpayers the opportunity to settle their tax debt for less than they owe. If paying your bill would create a true financial hardship, the IRS may allow you to negotiate that debt down to a more manageable amount. This is a long, difficult process but may be worth the effort if you would not be able to pay your tax bill even over time.

What counts as an undue hardship to the IRS? Proof that if you did pay the full tax amount on time you would be (for example): forced to sell a property at a sacrifice price, unable to pay your living expenses, evicted from your home, or forced to file for bankruptcy. IRS Form 1127 gives you an extension of time to pay your taxes, but not an extension of time to file your tax return. It also won't excuse you from late payment penalties or interest.

WHAT *NOT* TO DO IF YOU CAN'T PAY IN FULL

When people don't have enough money to cover their full tax bill and aren't aware of the IRS options, they often take actions that end up causing unnecessary financial harm. Some of the things you should avoid doing (if at all possible) in this circumstance include:

- Not filing a tax return, which subjects you to additional IRS penalties
- Putting the balance on a credit card, which always charges more interest than the IRS
- Borrowing from a 401(k) plan, which can cause a whole host of other financial problems
- Taking out a personal loan, which (again) probably comes with a bigger interest hit than the IRS plans

If you don't take any actions to pay your taxes, the IRS has the right to start enforced collection actions against you. That includes things like seizing your assets or placing liens on your property. For example, they could take your Social Security benefits, seize and sell your car, or garnish your wages. Plus, they can charge you penalties as big as 25% of the tax you originally owed. So, your best option here is to file your tax return on time and request one of the IRS payment options. As long as you stick to your agreement with the agency, they'll leave you alone.

IF YOU'RE A VICTIM OF IDENTITY THEFT

That's Not Me!

Any time someone uses your Social Security number along with other stolen personal information to file a false tax return and claim a refund, to claim other tax benefits, or to obtain work, you've been a victim of tax identity theft. Unfortunately, tax identity theft is on the rise. The IRS flagged more than one million returns for fraud suspicion during tax season 2023. The threat is so pervasive that the IRS has a special section on their website called "Identity Theft Central" to help taxpayers who are dealing with this issue.

In many cases, tax identity theft victims only find out what's happened when they try to file a tax return and the IRS won't accept it because they've already received a return with that Social Security number. Other times, there will be an IRS notice involved—an important reason to always open mail from the IRS.

SIGNS OF TAX IDENTITY THEFT

You won't know that you've been a victim of tax identity theft until after the fact, unfortunately. Some of the more common signs that someone has used your information include not being able to e-file your tax return, getting a letter from the IRS asking questions about a tax return that you didn't file, being notified by the IRS that an online account has been opened using your name, being unable to access your online IRS account, seeing that the IRS has records that show employers you didn't work for, or getting an IRS notice that you owe more tax for a return you haven't filed.

All of these indicate that someone has been using your name and Social Security number, and it can be a very difficult issue to fix. That's especially true if it takes you a long time to notice there's a problem and report it.

WHAT TO DO IF IT HAPPENS TO YOU

As soon as you realize you've been a victim of tax identity theft, report it immediately online at IdentityTheft.gov, courtesy of the Federal Trade Commission (FTC). Avoid other websites claiming that they can help solve this problem for you, as they're often phishing sites trying to get your information so they can take advantage of you too.

The official website (IdentityTheft.gov) can help you report the incident to all applicable agencies, create a fraud recovery plan, and put that plan into action. You can use this tool whether you've already been a victim or if you know someone has stolen your information and might use it fraudulently. The first step is to let the FTC know what happened, providing as many details as you can. The tool will then use that information to create an FTC Identity Theft Report and an IRS Identity Theft Affidavit (IRS Form 14039), which the FTC can then submit directly to the IRS if you want them to. Alternatively, you can complete Form 14039 yourself and submit it to the agency. Once the IRS receives your affidavit, they'll begin their investigation into your claim.

You can also opt for a personal recovery plan that will spell out all the other steps you may need to take and help track your progress. For example, with tax identity theft, you may also need to check your Social Security account to see if anyone has tried to claim benefits using your Social Security number.

If you've been unable to e-file your tax return due to tax identity theft, file a paper return. This will allow the IRS to process your real information while the investigation is taking place.

IDENTITY THEFT VICTIM ASSISTANCE

The IRS has a specialized team to help taxpayers deal with the fallout from tax identity theft called Identity Theft Victim Assistance (IDTVA). Once the agency receives your Identity Theft Affidavit, they'll assign your case to an employee who's been trained specifically to deal with this issue.

To help resolve your case, the IDTVA may look into whether this issue has affected more than one tax year, make sure your tax return gets processed properly, release your tax refund (if you were supposed to get one), remove the fraudulent tax return from your IRS records, mark your account with a special identity theft indicator to help protect you going forward, or analyze the case to make sure all of the outstanding issues have been taken care of.

Identity Protection PIN

An IRS Identity Protection PIN stops anyone else from filing a tax return with your Social Security number. The IRS assigns this to people who've been fraud victims, and once those cases are resolved the taxpayers will receive a new IP PIN every year by mail. These six-digit codes are available to anyone who wants them; you don't have to be a victim of tax identity theft to request one.

The IDTVA aims to resolve cases within 120 days, but your case may take longer depending on the circumstances and the case backlog. They will contact you when your case has been resolved, and let you know whether you will need to use an Identity Protection PIN moving forward.

PROTECTING YOURSELF AGAINST TAX IDENTITY THEFT

Untangling the mess of tax identity theft can be a frustrating, anxiety-provoking slog. Luckily, you can take steps to minimize the chances of it happening to you. Make sure to keep your Social Security number private, providing it to trusted parties only when it's absolutely necessary and keeping your physical card at home in a secure location. Watch out for phishing, vishing, and smishing scams where criminals try to trick you into giving out your personal information, sometimes posing as IRS officials. Also, be aware that the IRS will *never* contact you by phone, text, email, or social media; they will always contact you by regular USPS mail. File your taxes as early as you can, so no one else has the opportunity to file with your Social Security number. If you work with a paid tax preparer, check their credentials to make sure they're legit. Finally, consider getting an IRS Identity Protection PIN using the "Get an IP PIN" tool on the IRS website at www.irs.gov.

Taking these steps won't guarantee that you'll never be a victim of tax identity theft, but it will make it much less likely. Scammers are out there and they get sneakier all the time. It makes sense to do everything you can to get ahead of them and prevent a problem that can take months (even years) to solve.

IF YOU GET A NOTICE

Don't Burn after Reading

The most important thing you can do if you get a letter or notice from the IRS is to open it. Just seeing the IRS return address provokes fear and anxiety in many people, leading them to ignore the envelope or shove it to the bottom of a pile. But virtually all IRS communications come with deadlines, and missing those deadlines means you agree with the IRS by default. That can end up costing you a lot of money, even if it's money you don't really owe.

Your best option is to deal with any correspondence from the IRS as quickly as possible. Most notices are easy to clear up, but if your issue is more complicated, you can request additional time to respond. Bottom line: Don't wait; respond right away.

PAPERLESS PROCESSING INITIATIVE

Thanks to improvements made due to the Inflation Recovery Act, the IRS Paperless Processing Initiative allows taxpayers to respond to notices and submit other forms of correspondence online. This will be a huge help for taxpayers as they'll have quicker resolution for issues due to shorter processing time.

Historically, millions of taxpayers have had to send their responses, including detailed documentation, through the mail. IRS employees then have had to process those documents, leading to huge backlogs. In the meantime, people who responded to notices would get second and third notices for the same issue despite the fact they had replied to the IRS in a timely manner.

Along with this, the IRS launched its Simple Notice Initiative to make these notices easier for taxpayers to understand and comply with. Hundreds of IRS documents have been revamped, revised, and clarified, including the most common notices sent to taxpayers.

CP2000: THE MOST COMMON IRS NOTICE

The IRS sends out CP2000 (Notice of Underreported Income) notices when there's a mismatch between the numbers reported on your tax return and the information that they received from third parties (like on a W-2 or 1099). The difference may cause a change in your tax bill, and the IRS uses the CP2000 to explain their proposed change to your tax bill. These notices are extremely common, with the IRS sending millions of these every year. Sometimes you'll owe money; sometimes you'll end up getting money back.

If you get a CP2000, don't panic. These are extremely easy to resolve. Take these steps deal with your CP2000:

1. Read the entire notice.
2. Respond by the due date if you can or request an extension of time to respond.
3. If you agree with the IRS proposed changes, indicate that on the form, sign it, and follow the IRS instructions for actions to take.

If you don't agree with the IRS conclusion, you can dispute the notice. If you have the documentation you need, you'll send that in. If there's a mistake on the official documentation, like there's an error on your 1099, contact the provider and ask them to correct it, and include that with your response.

If you don't understand everything in the notice, you can contact the IRS for further explanation. There will be a toll-free number listed on the CP-2000 that you can call for assistance.

Some IRS Notices Are Wrong

Just because you got a notice from the IRS doesn't mean it's correct. If your records don't support the IRS conclusion, you have the opportunity to disagree with them. Explain why you disagree and provide any pertinent documentation with your response to their notice. They'll review it and resolve the issue.

DIFFERENT NOTICES FOR DIFFERENT ISSUES

The IRS has a different notice for practically every situation you can think of. They're all numbered, and each comes with the computer paragraph (CP) tag. Most taxpayers won't see most of these notices, but it's still good to know what each covers in case you get one. You can find the notice number on either the top right or bottom right of your letter from the IRS.

Here are some of the most common notices for individual (as opposed to business) taxpayers:

- **CP09, Earned Income Credit You May Be Entitled To:** sent to taxpayers who could have claimed the earned income tax credit (EITC) but didn't
- **CP11, Changes in Tax Return, Balance Due:** where the IRS corrected your tax return and you owe money

- **CP12, Changes in Tax Return, Overpayment:** where the IRS corrected your tax return and they owe you money
- **CP23, Estimated Tax Payment Discrepancy with Balance Due:** when your reported estimated tax payments don't match what the IRS has posted to your account and you owe some money
- **CP59, You Didn't File a Tax Return:** which the IRS sends when they haven't received a return from you for a particular tax year
- **CP161, Balance Due Request for Payment:** where you have an unpaid balance that needs to be addressed
- **CP180/181, Missing Form or Schedule:** which is a notification that a tax return can't be processed because at least one necessary form or schedule was not included with the return
- **CP521, Reminder of Installment Payment:** which is a notification that there's a payment due on an IRS tax payment plan
- **CP523, Default on Installment Agreement—IRS Intent to Terminate Agreement and Seize Assets:** where payments have not been made on an installment agreement and the IRS will place a levy on assets

No matter what type of notice you receive, open the envelope right away. Go through your records to see whether or not they support the IRS conclusion. And, most important, make sure to follow the instructions in the notice and respond before the deadline. If you can't handle it on your own, have a tax professional help you deal with the notice.

BEWARE FAKE IRS NOTICES

Identity theft scammers often pose as the IRS, tricking unsuspecting taxpayers into revealing personal information and sending money in hopes of avoiding IRS actions. Once they have your Social Security number and other identifying data, they can do a lot more than file fake tax returns to swipe your refund.

First, remember that the IRS will never contact you by phone, text, email, or through social media. First contact will be through the mail, but that doesn't even slow scammers down. Here are some signs of fraudulent IRS notices: spelling and grammar mistakes, missing the IRS logo, incorrect name or address, sentences that don't sound quite right, threatening language, demands for immediate payment, requests for cash payments or gift cards, and requests for banking or credit card information.

If you do get an IRS notice that seems suspicious, log in to your online IRS account. Real notices will be available in your account. You can also call IRS taxpayer service by calling 1-800-829-1040.

IF YOU GET AUDITED

Bring Your Receipts

Even the thought of getting audited can strike fear in the hearts of American taxpayers, but it's honestly not as bad as most people imagine. If your tax return gets selected for audit, the IRS will contact you by mail. The most important thing to do is open the letter and start planning for your response.

Contrary to popular belief, audits don't usually end with huge tax bills, IRS levies, or jail time. They rarely involve a face-to-face meeting with an IRS auditor. In many cases, there's no change to the taxes at all; sometimes the IRS just needs more information. Other times you could end up owing money or getting a refund. And if you disagree with their findings, you can appeal the decision. You have more power here than you may realize.

CORRESPONDENCE AUDITS

Some audits are initiated and resolved by mail, meaning no need for face time with an IRS agent. There are two basic types of correspondence audits: notices like the CP-2000 and audit letters. Notices like CP-2000 are called simple letters, and are mainly used to clear up math errors, reporting mismatches, and accidental omissions (like some interest income you forgot to include on your tax return).

Audit letters call for more on your part. They're sent when the IRS wants backup for something claimed on your tax return. These requests for documentation don't mean you did something wrong. They just mean the IRS is looking for corroboration for a deduction you took: an acknowledgment letter from a charitable organization or medical expense receipts, for example. Submitting your documentation usually resolves the issue quickly. If you don't have documentation, your deductions could be disallowed, increasing both your taxable income and taxes due.

What's Your Audit Risk?

With expanded funding from the Inflation Reduction Act, the IRS plans to increase enforcement actions—and that means more audits. As of 2024, only about 1% of returns get audited, but the agency is looking to beef up those numbers. Their first focus appears to be high-income taxpayers. The best defense: Be honest on your tax return and keep the receipts.

OFFICE AUDITS

When the IRS has questions about your tax return that are too big or complicated for a correspondence audit, they may ask you to come in for an office audit. These audits usually involve more issues and are often tied to Schedule A (Itemized Deductions), Schedule C (Profit of Loss from Business—Sole Proprietorship), or Schedule E (Supplemental Income and Loss—from Rental Properties, Royalties, Partnerships, S corporations, etc.). The audit may start based on information on one of these schedules, and quickly grow to encompass other forms and schedules from the return.

The IRS will send you a letter asking you to come to a specific IRS office during a preset appointment time, which you can reschedule if needed. You are allowed to bring your tax professional to represent you, and this can help keep the audit on track and limit the scope of the inquiry. People who go on their own may share more information than they need to, leading to additional questions by the IRS.

FIELD AUDITS

Field audits are the most nerve-wracking for taxpayers, where specialized IRS revenue agents come to your home or place of business to examine your records. These comprehensive audits are relatively rare and are conducted by highly trained IRS agents. Unlike other types of audits, these are not limited in scope. The agent (or agents) will review records, conduct interviews, and look around the home or business facility. The audits can be intrusive and feel daunting for taxpayers.

Field audits can take anywhere from a day to several weeks. This depends on how complicated the tax issues and records are, what the auditors learn from interviews and record reviews, and how cooperative the taxpayer is. To protect yourself and your rights, you should have a tax attorney present during a field audit.

COMPLIANCE AUDITS

National Research Program (NRP) audits look at the returns of randomly selected taxpayers to determine their level of voluntary compliance with tax law. These dreaded line-by-line audits are conducted occasionally (not every tax year) to add information to the IRS databases. That data helps the IRS figure out target areas for future directed audits. It also helps them identify areas that taxpayers may have difficulty complying with or that require additional clarification from the agency.

Still, the subjected taxpayers have to suffer through a detailed audit of their tax returns. Many of these audits result in additional taxes, interest, and penalties.

COMMON AUDIT TRIGGERS

The IRS doesn't want to waste time or money on unproductive audits. They go for returns that are most likely to end up netting them more tax dollars. That means a focus on returns with lots of deductions, possibly ineligible tax credits, and higher-income taxpayers. That doesn't mean you shouldn't take all allowable deductions and credits you qualify for. It does mean that you should be aware of the audit potential and keep very good records.

Returns that may face a higher audit risk include business or rental losses, underreported income, claiming the Earned Income Tax Credit or the Child Tax Credit, earnings greater than $500,000 per year, earnings less than $20,000 per year, owning digital assets like cryptocurrency, numbers that don't make sense (such as round numbers for all business expenses), and deductions that don't fit with your income (like $15,000 in donations on a $40,000 salary).

Generally, the IRS can audit the last three years of tax returns. But if they find substantial errors, they may go back as far as six years.

WHEN TO GET HELP

Most taxpayers can resolve CP-2000 notices on their own. For anything more in-depth than that, it's probably worth at least talking with a tax professional. If you paid someone to prepare your return, they can usually help with notices and will typically charge for this additional service. If you did your own return but used paid tax prep software, you may have access to audit support from that.

But when it comes to dealing with the IRS in person, you'll want a tax professional to be right there with you. They will talk to the IRS on your behalf, helping make sure that you don't say anything out of nervousness that could open you up to more issues with the agency. In fact, unless the IRS specifically requests your presence, your representative can attend meetings without you.

If you have met with the IRS yourself, you can still request representation and that will generally stop the interview process. Several types of professionals may represent taxpayers in front of the IRS including certified public accountants (CPAs), enrolled agents (EAs), tax attorneys, and enrolled actuaries.

In order to have someone represent you, you must sign a Power of Attorney allowing it before they can have any contact with the IRS on your behalf. You can find tax professionals in your area by searching the Directory of Federal Tax Return Preparers with Credentials and Select Qualifications on the IRS website at ww.irs.gov.

ACKNOWLEDGMENTS

I want to thank Eileen and Jennifer for always making me a better writer. And Shine and Annie, who helped me gather tons of information and found some superinteresting tax facts. And Jenny, who always has my back.

INDEX